GUILIN

China's Masterpiece

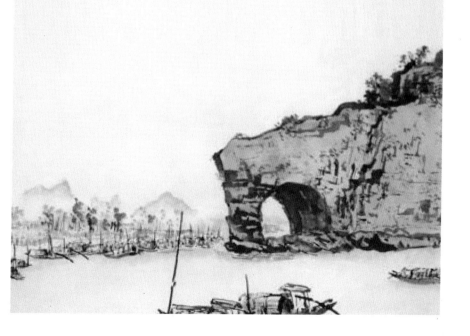

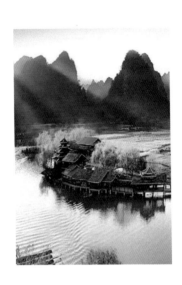

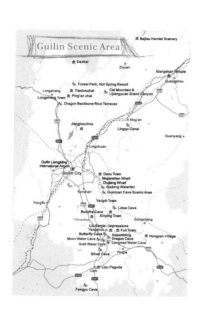

Guilin Scenic Area

Bajiao Hamlet Scenery

Dezhai

Ziyuan

Xiangshan Temple

Guangzhou

Forest Park, Hot Spring Resort

Longsheng
Longsheng Town

Tiantouzhai
Ping'an zhai

Cat Mountain &
Lijiangyuan Grand Canyon

Dragon Backbone Rice Terraces

Xing'an

Jiangtouzhou

Lingqu Canal

Guanyang

Lingchuan

Guilin Liangjiang
International Airport

Guilin City

Daxu Town
Mopanshan Wharf
Zhujiang Wharf
Gudong Waterfall
Guanyan Cave Scenic Area

Yongfu

Yanshan

Yangdi Town

Lotus Cave

Buddha Cave

Xinping Town

Yulong River

Gongcheng

Liu Sanjie · Impressions
Yangshuo

Full Town

Butterfly Cave
Moon Water Cave
Gold Water Cave

Assembling
Dragon Cave
Longmen Water Cave

Hongyan Village

Silver Cave

Pingle

Lipu Pagoda

Lipu

Fengyu Cave

1. Guilin.

One of China's most scenic tourist cities, Guilin is situated at the start of an idyllic stretch of the Li River, with karst mountains providing a beguiling backdrop. The beautiful city is threaded by two rivers and four lakes and studded by karst mountains. Many hurry onto Yangshuo but Guilin, ancient seat of the Jinjiang kings, has enough of interest to merit a longer stay.

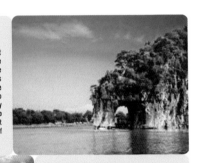

2. Dragon's Backbone Rice Terraces.

This once isolated area is now one of the Southwest's most recognisable tourist attractions. It is the steeply terraced fields that have earned this county its illustrative name. When the paddy fields fill with water in springtime, they glitter in the sunlight, giving an ethereal quality to the spectacular scene. There are famous mountains and ethnic minority villages to discover in all directions.

3. The Li River.

The Li River is the Guilin centrepiece; synonymous with the bucolic scenery it has sculpted for eons. Part of an historic system of waterways, the generally shallow and sometimes steep sided Li flows through villages and bamboo forests. Some part of its winding jade waters, flanked by lurching karst mountains, will be included in any given Yangshuo postcard.

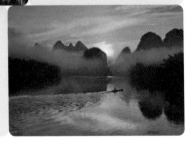

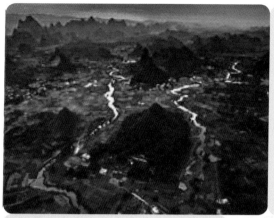

4. Yangshuo.

The bustle on Yangshuo's main thorough fare, the pedestrianised walking street of West Street, is just a testament to its popularity as one of China's top tourism draws. Idyllic Yangshuo nestles on the east bank of the meandering Li River near the confluence with the Yulong River. Only a short distance outside the township, Yangshuo County still possesses the allure of its natural scenery and rural life.

5. Outer Counties.

Guilin and Yangshuo are tourist towns par excellence but increasingly, travellers are exploring further afield, as new roads make the other eight counties of Guilin more accessible. From the 1000-year old village of Jiangtouzhou to the extraordinary danxia rock formations of the Bajiao gorge, there are little known gems and historic wonders, that if you've the time to spend, are well worth checking out.

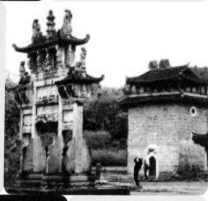

6. Directories.

Whatever you look for in Guilin, you will find information about it here. Learn about local festivals and rural gueshouses. Discover the best places in Guilin and Yangshuo to try Beer Fish or Guilin Rice Noodles. Find the ideal location to charter a city bike or enjoy a wild night out.

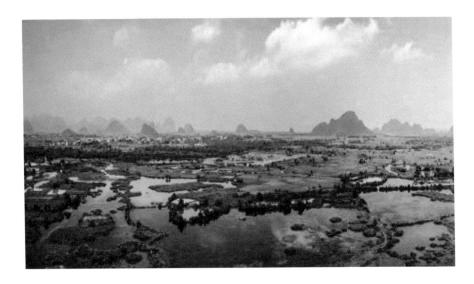

CONTENTS

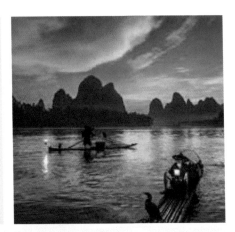

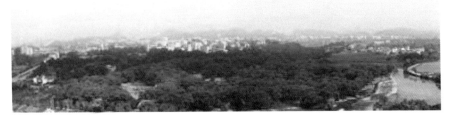

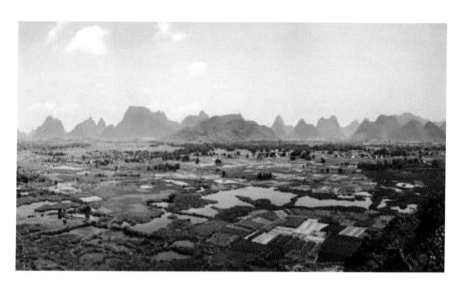

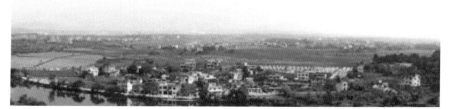

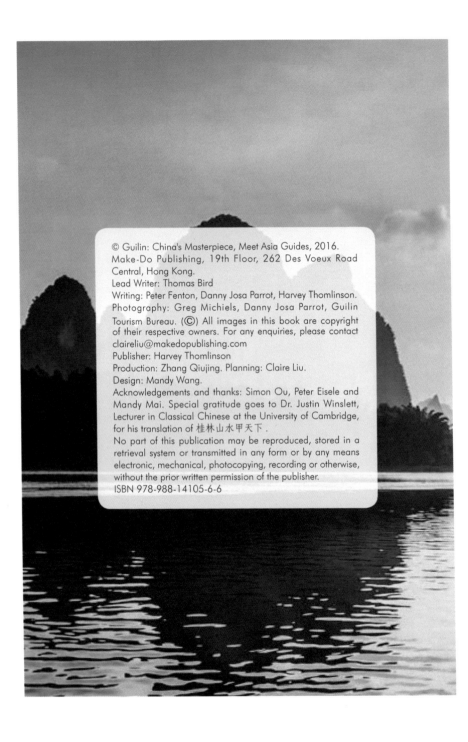

© Guilin: China's Masterpiece, Meet Asia Guides, 2016.
Make-Do Publishing, 19th Floor, 262 Des Voeux Road
Central, Hong Kong.
Lead Writer: Thomas Bird
Writing: Peter Fenton, Danny Josa Parrot, Harvey Thomlinson.
Photography: Greg Michiels, Danny Josa Parrot, Guilin
Tourism Bureau. (©) All images in this book are copyright of
their respective owners. For any enquiries, please contact
claireliu@makedopublishing.com
Publisher: Harvey Thomlinson
Production: Zhang Qiujing. Planning: Claire Liu.
Design: Mandy Wang.
Acknowledgements and thanks: Simon Ou, Peter Eisele and
Mandy Mai. Special gratitude goes to Dr. Justin Winslett,
Lecturer in Classical Chinese at the University of Cambridge,
for his translation of 桂林山水甲天下.

ISBN 978-988-14105-6-6

Thomas Bird

Thomas is an itinerant writer lost in Asia who occasionally prints his musings in the Guardian, Lonely Planet Online and other publications. He has contributed to several guidebooks including Rough Guides China and Dunhuang: A City on the Silk Road. You can follow his journey at www.thomasbird.info

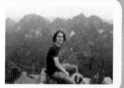

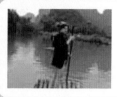

Danny Josa Parrott

Danny studied Oriental Studies at the University of Oxford. before in 2009 he set off on an ambitious round the world adventure. Nowadays he devotes his time to arranging volunteering opportunities in China (check out his website, www.go-to.co).

Peter Fenton

Peter is an experienced writer whose travel pieces have appeared in a variety of publications. Originally from Australia, he lived in Guangzhou for over five years and often visited Guilin. Peter contributed the hiking and climbing sections to our Guilin guide.

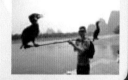

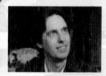

Harvey Thomlinson

Harvey is publisher of Meet Asia guides and has contributed to many China travel titles, including Ancient China Villages. Harvey's press Make-Do Publishing also translates and publishes fiction by authors from around Asia.

Zhang Qiujing

Zhang Qiujing is the founder of Beijing Jinghan Cultural Media, a partner of Meet China guides. Qiujing has extensive experience in China travel and she co-produced our Dunhuang and Guilin guidebooks.

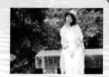

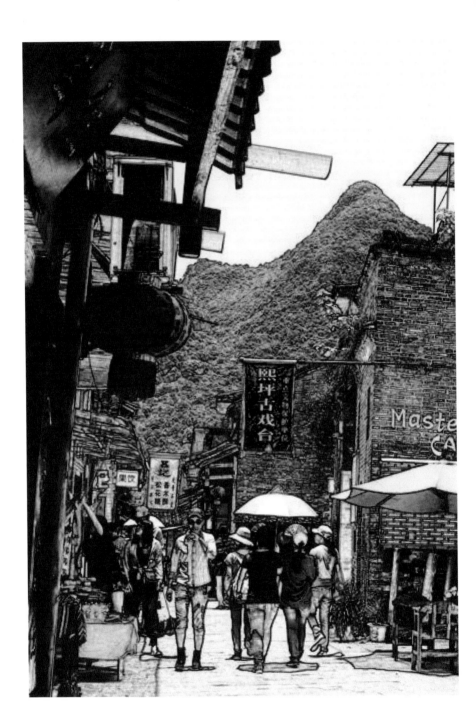

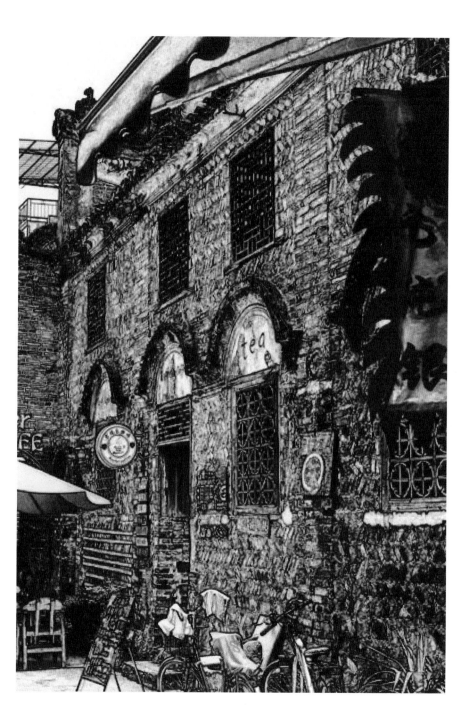

1 Overview

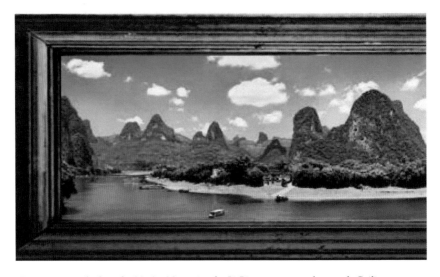

From its source high in the Mao'er Mountains the Li River sweeps south towards Guilin and into the world's imagination. The karst scenery, rich cultural tapestry, and superb hiking, biking, climbing and caving have made Guilin south China's top travel destination.

EULOGISED by poets and artists, the 83km stretch of the Li River between Guilin and Yangshuo threads a picturebook of karsk peaks, ancient villages and brushstroke bamboo. For centuries Guilin, once a remote outpost of empire but now the third-largest city in **Guangxi** province, has been acclaimed for its scenery. A Song dynasty (960-1279) governor of Guangxi, Wang Zhenggong described Guilin's river and hills as '**the best in the realm**' and they have become synonymous with an ideal of Chinese landscape beauty.

Travellers are drawn above all by the fantastic **karst landscape** reflected in the Li River's limpid green waters. The outer-skin of the limestone peaks has been washed away through millennia of water erosion leaving a fairytale landscape of allusion. Guilin's karst topography not only extends to the spectacular pinnacles above ground, but also to **caves** and **waterways** under the surface of the earth. So other-worldly is the Guilin scenery, that the Li River was selected as a location for the Wookiee planet in the film **Star Wars: Revenge of the Sith**.

Since the 1980s, Guilin's reputation for pastoral beauty has made it one of China's biggest hits with foreign visitors. The county town of **Yangshuo** on the banks of the Li soon emerged as the base for travellers bent on adventures in the surrounding countryside. Over time, Yangshuo's laid-back vibe has drawn more Chinese tourists. As Yangshuo fills up, the independent traveller scene is now moving on to the countryside, where characterful resorts are being wrought from restored farmhouses.

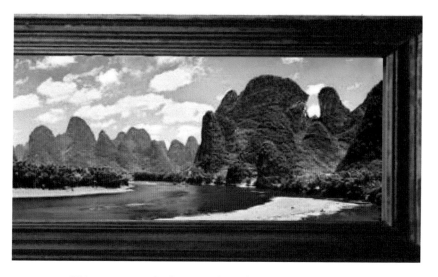

Visitors may come for the scenery but Guilin's form as a travel destination goes far beyond this. The region is a paradise for **outdoor activities** enthusiasts, with the **Yulong** River valley near Yangshuo a sublime spot for cycling, hiking and boating. Meanwhile Yangshuo has also emerged as one of Asia's top **climbing** destinations, with over 800 routes for all levels of climbers, and the karst hills offer intrepid caving adventures.

History lovers will discover plenty to intrigue them. The Guilin area's position as an historic highway between the central plains and the south has left a tangible cultural legacy in the string of ancient river towns along the Li river including **Daxu**, **Xingping** and **Fuli**. In **Xing'an County** is the **Lingqu canal**, one of the world's oldest human-made waterways, built two-thousand years ago by the first Qin emperor (247BCE-220BCE).

Another fascination are the **ethnic minority** peoples who inhabit what was in ancient times a wild area on the western edges of empire. Guangxi province's official name is the **Guangxi Zhuang Autonomous Region** on account of the large number of Zhuang people, but many rare ethnic groups live in what was once known as 'the land of one hundred tribes'. The spectacular **Longji Rice Terraces**, 100km north of Guilin are a popular place to trek between Yao, Zhuang and Miao villages and encounter diverse cultures which shaped the history of this region.

Whatever brings you to Guilin, it's the incomparable scenery of the Li River that provides the setting for your travel experience. If you feel like getting off the beaten track, the outlying counties contain more natural wonders, from the impressive Danxia landscape at **Baijiao Mountain Fortress**, to **Cat Mountain** (Mao'er Shan). Small wonder that many visitors stay longer than expected, return often, and even end up relocating to live their Guilin dream.

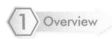

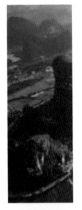

Cultural Significance

Guilin scenery is considered symbolic of the beauty of Chinese landscapes. Paintings of Guilin adorn conference rooms and hotel lobbies across China and Guilin's significance received the ultimate endorsement when the Li River scenery was featured on the **20 yuan banknote**.

Centuries of cultured visitors have memorialised Guilin. The hills around Guilin are adorned by etchings of lyric songs, poetic essays, epigraphs and couplets made by visiting literati. 213 of these can be found in **Guilin Tablets Forest**, with the earliest dating back to Tang times. Guilin also had an influence on the evolution of Chinese landscape painting, through the works of masters like **Mifu**, and in the twentieth century it has spawned its own 'Li River Painting School.'

Guilin city itself has a glorious cultural heritage. The 630 year old **Jingjiang Prince's Palace**, home to generations of local kings from Ming times, is older than the Forbidden City. The **Jinjiang Mausoleum** is the largest King mausoleum in China. Guilin also holds the imprint of twentieth century history, from sites associated with the Red Army's **Long March**, to the city's links with the legendary **Flying Tigers**, American airmen who fought with Chinese against Japan.

Given these natural and cultural riches, Guilin ranks highly among Chinese tourist cities. As early as 1973, Guilin was officially opened to international tourism—U.S. Presidents Nixon and Clinton were among a long line of VIPs to be brought here—and by 1984, the city was proclaimed one of China's twenty-four 'historical and cultural cities'. Indeed, Guilin is a 'key tourist city' of not just Guangxi but all of China, as its fabled landscape helps attract international tourists to the Middle Kingdom.

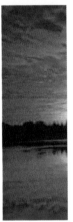

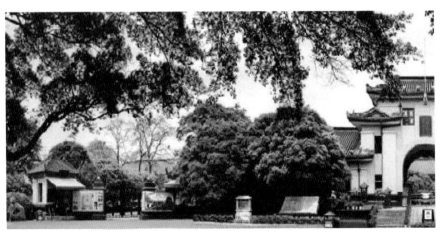

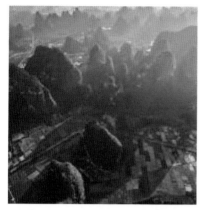

Visiting and Orientation

On the banks of the Li River, the scenic low-rise city of Guilin is home to the region's only **international airport** and is where many visitors will arrive by plane or high-speed train. The city has welcomed travellers for centuries and offers a broad range of hotels and restaurants to suit most budgets. Local tourist attractions sculpted from the city's hills include **Seven Stars Park**, **Prince's City**, **Folded Brocade Hill**, and **Elephant Hill Park**.

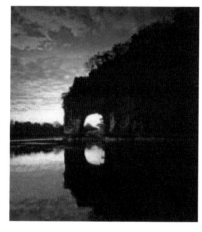

Guilin city is divided into six districts while the surrounding countryside comprises nine counties and two autonomous counties. 80km downstream along the Li River, the laid back county town of **Yangshuo** is the true capital of local tourism, the gateway to a beautiful world of attractions in the countryside. Many visitors base themselves in the backpacker mecca of **West Street** while they indulge their enthusiasm for biking, boating, or hiking, and exploring old villages and towns, particularly those along the idyllic **Yulong River**. As Yangshuo fills up with Chinese tourists, many visitors are relocating into the surrounding countryside and taking less developed towns like **Xingping** as their base.

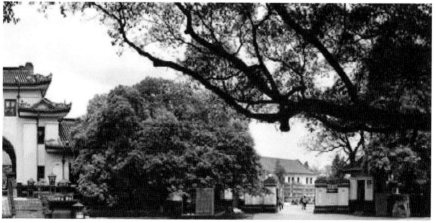

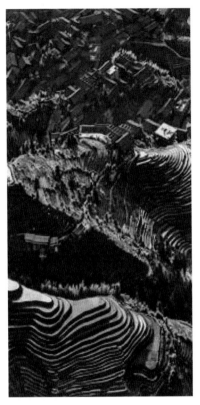

The most popular way to travel between the Li River tourist hubs of Guilin and Yangshuo is to ride one of the diesel-guzzling tourist boats, which offer close-up views of the most exquisite stretch of the river with its landmarks such as **Nine Horses Picture Hill**. Other tourists start downstream at **Yangdi** for a combination of hiking or motorised rafting and a more intimate experience of the river. Another major draw are ancient towns along the Li River such as Fuli and Xinping.

However the Guilin-Yangshuo Li river axis is by no means the whole picture as there is much to explore in the **outer counties**. 100km to the northwest of Guilin, the remarkable step formations of the **Longji Rice Terraces** are now one of southwest China's most recognisable tourist attractions. Many tourists spend two or three days here hiking and experiencing the area's fascinating minority cultures. While Guilin, Yangshuo and Longji are well known, increasingly curious travellers are exploring further afield. If you have the time, a little persistence will uncover little known gems that are well worth checking out. Beyond Guilin and Yangshuo, the local tourism infrastructure is still under development meaning that visitors should improvise to get the most out of their experience.

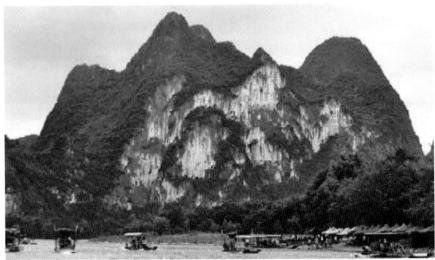

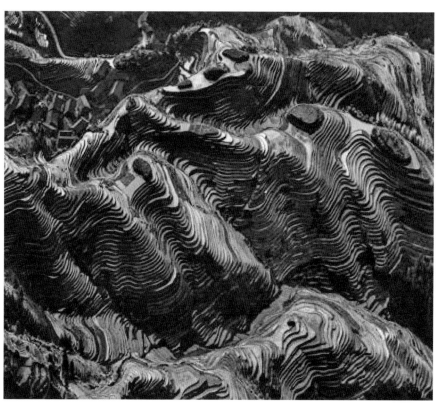

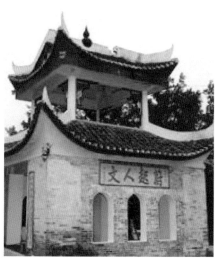

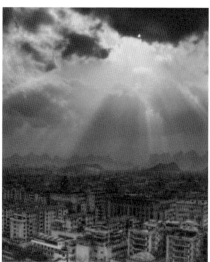

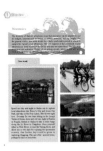

Two weeks

If you have another week, you might enjoy an extra day in Guilin visiting sights in the surrounding area such as Yao Mountain and Crown Cave, then hike or boat from Yangdi to Xingping, and extend your Yangshuo sojourn with hiking, boating, caving and climbing.

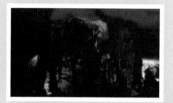

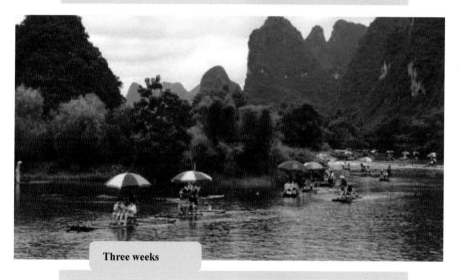

Three weeks

A longer stay creates opportunities to make for the outer counties and explore off the beaten path attractions like Jiangtouzhou or Cat Mountain. However another option would to kick back in Yangshuo and perhaps enroll in classes such as taiji, cooking, and chinese languge.

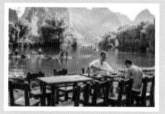

History:

History lovers could plan a trip based around attractions like Prince's City and the **Jinjiang Mausoleum** in Guilin, and ancient Li River towns like Daxu, Xingping and Fuli. There are also interesting sites in the outer counties, like **Zhouwei Temple** in **Gongcheng built** in the year 178, and **Xiangshan Temple** (湘 山 寺) in Quanzhou County.

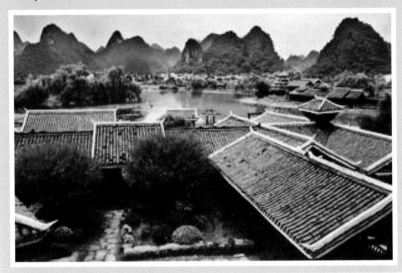

Outdoor Activities:

The Guilin area offers great cycling, boating and hiking. Many of the most scenic locations for these activities are around the Yulong River near Yangshuo. You will find more information and maps of some of the best routes in Chapter Five. For the Yangdi to Xingping Li River hike see page 71.

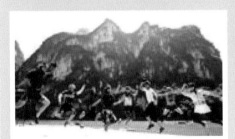
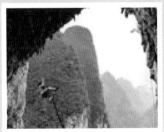

Climbers could spend a lifetime mastering the 800 routes around Yangshuo. The area's popularity is based upon the many and varied routes. You can find an introduction to Yangshuo climbing on pages 95-101. Meanwhile Yangshuo also offers a vast array of caves to explore, from illuminated show cases, to the labyrinthine Buddha Cave and the Longmen Water Cave. See pages 102-108.

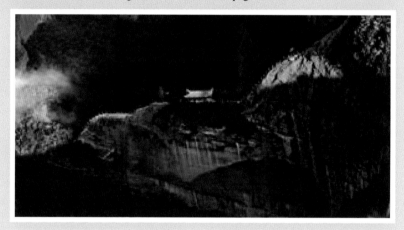

Scenery:

Those in search of great scenery to photograph or just enjoy, after sating themselves wih the glories of the Li and Yulong rivers, might head for the danxia formations of **Baijiao Mountain Fortress** (where it is possible to cross from Guangxi into Hunan), or **Cat Mountain**.

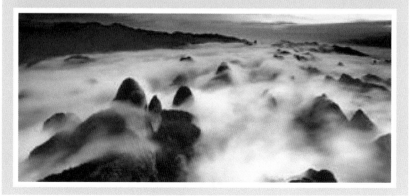

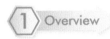

Environment & Climate

Guilin has a monsoon-influenced, subtropical climate. Precipitation is above 1,900 mm annually (that's more than the UK) and over 50% of that is delivered through April and June. The **peak tourist months** of July and August are also pretty wet, though these are paradoxically the sunniest months as rain comes in sudden downpours, making flooding a sporadic problem. These months are also very **humid**, which can make getting around seriously sweaty business. Autumn and winter are comparatively drier and cooler.

The Li River delights in all four seasons, although April to October are the most popular months to visit because of the warmer weather. August sees highs that reach into the mid-30s, so pack some sun lotion if you're planning on getting out and about. Summer is when Yangshuo's West Street becomes a surging human sea. Outside peak season the crowds are smaller and prices often lower, while the karst hills brood in mist. Be warned though that Guilin winters and springs can be damp. January is the coldest month on average with the mercury dipping as low as five degrees centigrade (pretty nippy considering there's no central heating).

While China's contribution to global warming is well documented, Guilin is a **protected region** where polluting industry is forbidden. Air and water quality remain good by Chinese standards, though construction, particularly in the booming tourist sector, has made noise and dust an annoyance in select areas.

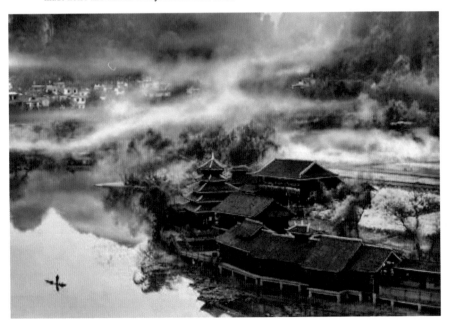

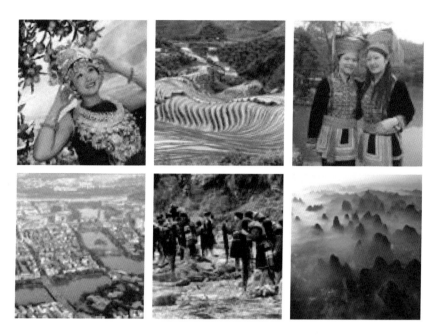

Population & People

Guilin was long a human crossroads on the trade route that developed between the southern borderlands and **Hunan** province. The city was until relatively recently the capital of **Guangxi**, one of China's most ethnically diverse regions. This has influenced the cosmopolitan makeup of Guilin folk. In the twentieth century there was a major influx of northern Chinese fleeing the Japanese during World War Two. Since economic reforms in the 1980s, outsiders have continued to arrive, attracted by the serene environment or work opportunities in the tourist industry. The influence of Hunan, Guilin's neighbour to the north, is evident in the popularity of spicy food.

Guilin's diverse human tapestry is a major draw for visitors. Guangxi province's official name is the **Guangxi Zhuang Autonomous Region** on account of the large number of Zhuang people who live in this ancient frontier zone. You'll even see what appear to be misspelled signs on prominent buildings. In fact, this is the Romanization of the Zhuang language. So the name of the province actually appears as Gvangjsih Bouxchengh Swcigih. Good luck pronouncing that.

Almost five million people call Guilin their home, including Zhuang, Yao, Miao, Hui, Dong and Han people. Of these, a little under one million live in the city itself with the rest inhabiting outlying counties. One of the most popular places to explore minority cultures are in the villages of the stunning Longji Rice terraces (see pages 57-58.)

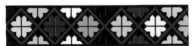

Ethnic Minorities

Yao people

Yao people are also prevalent in Guilin and their appearance and dress is far more distinct than the Zhuang's, especially that of the Red Yao in Longsheng, who don't cut their hair and sport big, hooped earrings. The Yao people have long been troublesome residents of the Chinese Empire. They were first pushed from their homelands in Hunan and fled southwards into Guangdong, Guangxi, Yunnan and Southeast Asia, then up into remote mountainous areas. One of the bloodiest battles in Guangxi's history was that at Big Rattan Gorge when the Yao fought the Zhuang in 1465. The Yao were also complicit in the Miao rebellions that so troubled the Ming Empire. A Yao revolt in 1831 is widely seen as a precursor to the extraordinarily destructive Taiping Rebellion in 1850. The Yao's resistance to Han dominion lasted until relatively recently, despite the Party's best efforts to integrate them through favourable policies and propaganda. Ironically, it is the trappings of globalisation, technology, infrastructure and mass tourism that are finally drawing the Yao into the modern world. Guilin has one Yao autonomous county, Gongcheng, just east of Yangshuo, and several autonomous Yao towns to explore.

Zhuang people

The **Zhuang people**, with an estimated population of 18 million, are the largest ethnic minority in China and make up 32% of Guangxi's entire population. They are highly integrated into mainstream Chinese life and difficult to tell apart from the Han Chinese in urban areas. In rural areas it's a different story and Guilin still has plenty of towns and villages where the Zhuang persist as they have for centuries, speaking their local version of the Zhuang language, the women still wearing traditional dresses. They are particularly visible in **Ping'an** in **Longsheng County** and various restaurants still advertise classic Zhuang cuisine, typically salty and sour dishes served with pickles, pork and dried fish.

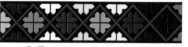

Miao people

The **Miao people** are also prevalent in Guilin, particularly around **Liangshui**, just north of **Mao'er Mountain**. Like the Yao, the Miao are found across south China and Southeast Asia and have distinctive dress, language and culture and are known for their unique song and dance routines and silver jewellery. They arrived in Guangxi during the Yuan Dynasty and have proved equally difficult to sinolise.

The most popular places to explore minority cultures are the villages of the stunning Longji Rice terraces (see pages 57-58.) In Guilin city, the main exhibition at the Guilin Museum provides a helpful introduction (see page 46).

Other minorities

Adding to this eclectic ethnological landscape, there are also packets of **Dong people**, famed for their sweet rice, and Muslim **Hui people** scattered around Guilin. The latter of which even has an autonomous town, **Caoping Hui Autonomous Town** on the Li River. The local dialect Guilinhua is a member of the Southwest branch of Mandarin, though standard Mandarin is widely spoken. You'll also hear a number of rural sub-dialects and ethnic minority languages. A sizeable minority of people understand Cantonese, the language spoken in the provincial capital **Nanning** and neighbouring **Guangdong Province**. English is spoken to varying degrees of fluency in tourist areas, particularly **Yangshuo**.

Despite the city's mixed heritage, locals maintain a discernable regional character, language and eating culture. They tend to be relaxed and lifestyle orientated as a rule, with limited concern for politics of the day. Most folk are friendly and accustomed to helping travellers but the area's status as a top tourist destination (and chronic regional wealth disparities) has cultivated a reputation for cheating, so be on guard for inflated "foreigner" prices and pickpockets.

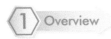

Economy

In 2013, **Guilin's** GDP was worth RMB165 billion with a GDP per capita of RMB31,774. Tourism is very much the main support of the local economy. In 2014, about 3,870,000 tourists travelled to Guilin including 203,000 international tourists, a number which was up five per cent on the previous year. Guilin has built up tourism sector facilities, including an extensive transportation network, which generated approximately RMB6.2 billion in revenue for the local economy that year.

The importance of tourism to local communities can hardly be overestimated. As far back as the Tang dynasty tourism was evident in Guilin attracting the political establishment and scholars from around China. It is estimated that two million Guilin locals now earn their living from the Li River, which is now worked by more than 300 tourist boats. The spectacular **Impressions: Liu Sanjie show** performed on the Li River at Yangshuo employs a cast of 600 locals.

Unlike other famed Chinese tourist destinations, Guilin doesn't otherwise have a diversified economic base with **Nanning** and **Liuzhou** sustaining Guangxi's industrial sector. Together with **tourism, agriculture** is a mainstay, however the economy is modernising with Guilin's emerging seven pillars of manufacturing as well as the more established tertiary education sector and handicrafts.

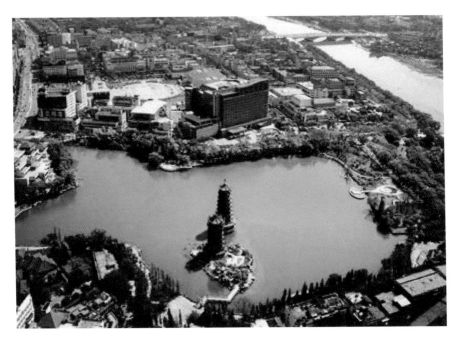

History

Guilin's first history books were its limestone hills. History and legend are inscribed in the karst, from Tang literati travelogues to rock drawings of fishing and hunting scenes. The prehistoric remains of the **Baoji cave people** rewind the Guilin history tape about 30,000 years.

During the historical period, Guilin was long a contested space on the ragged eastern edges of empire. Bleeding into a politically fluid **Yunnan** to the west, the area was dominated by non-Han tribes, including the majority **Zhuang**. In 214B the Yellow Emperor **Qin Shihuang** (221BCE – 20BCE) set up camp here during his campaign's against the Nanyue kingdom. Qin built the **Lingqu Canal** that established Guilin as a gateway between the Central plains of the Yangtze river and the **Lingnan** area.

The foundation of **Shi An County** during the Eastern Han Dynasty (25 – 220) is considered a direct precursor of modern Guilin. Shi An county, also called **Lingui** during Tang times (618-907), became an important southern prefecture. Armies were dispatched to guard the southwest border and canals built to transport grain from the central plains. The empire's peril was underlined during the late Tang when Zhuang tribes cut a deadly deal with Yunnan's **Southern Zhao Kingdom**. The alliance split Guangxi into a western half under Zhuang control, and an eastern bloc under the imperial yoke.

In 971, armies of the Song (960-971) secured the whole area and gave birth to Guangxi province, which was extended as far as today's Hainan island. Fragments of the Song city wall still survive in downtown Guilin (see page 44). Meanwhile the banks of Mulong Hu are clustered with nouveau Song architecture, symbolising the importance of this era for the city's development.

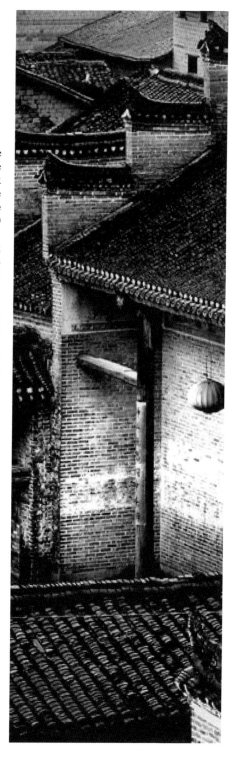

Song Tourism Boom

During the Song dynasty, newly pacified Guilin's scenery won empire-wide fame. Visiting Guilin became fashionable with Song literati and there are contemporary descriptions of sightseers in chariots causing traffic jams on local roads. Some 22 of 43 stone inscriptions of Elephant Trunk Hill are of Song provenance, along with 111 of the 213 from Guihua Tablets Forest, and 79 of 261 in Putao Mountain. Solitary Beauty Peak has a famous inscription from a poem by Song governor Wang Zhenggang: *'Guilin's landscape is best in the realm'.* This is still used by Guilin as its unofficial slogan. The Ming age saw a second peak in Guilin tourism as measured by dating of local inscriptions, counting for 42 of the tablets in Guihai Tablets Forest, 46 inscriptions on Putao Mountain and 47 on Solitary Beauty Peak.

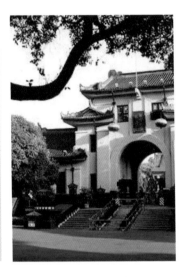

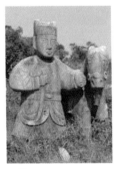

Guilin's political and economic importance waxed during the Ming (1364-1644) and Qing (1644-1911) eras. Under the reign of the local **Jingjiang kings** in the late 14th century, the city reached peak influence. Located in Solitary Beauty Park, the ancient **Mansion of Prince Jingjiang** is not only a record of Ming Guilin but one of the best preserved prince's palaces of that period (see page 37). The funky brick pagoda on Elephant Trunk Hill is also of Ming vintage (see page 35).

During the Qing dynasty, Guilin became considered a centre of Lingnan culture, even though Lingnan is associated principally with Guangdong. Local artists helped to spread the fame of its scenery which continued to attract cultured travellers. Meanwhile Qing Guilin is the background to the famous story of **Liu Sanjie**, a young girl fated to battle the class divisions of the landlord society (see page 86).

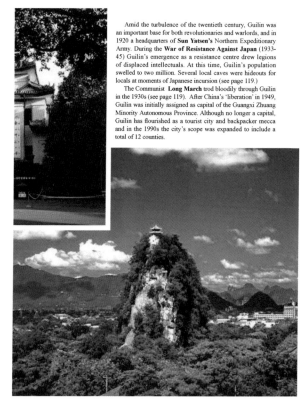

Amid the turbulence of the twentieth century, Guilin was an important base for both revolutionaries and warlords, and in 1920 a headquarters of **Sun Yatsen's** Northern Expeditionary Army. During the **War of Resistance Against Japan** (1933-45) Guilin's emergence as a resistance centre drew legions of displaced intellectuals. At this time, Guilin's population swelled to two million. Several local caves were hideouts for locals at moments of Japanese incursion (see page 119.)

The Communist **Long March** trod bloodily through Guilin in the 1930s (see page 119). After China's 'liberation' in 1949, Guilin was initially assigned as capital of the Guangxi Zhuang Minority Autonomous Province. Although no longer a capital, Guilin has flourished as a tourist city and backpacker mecca and in the 1990s the city's scope was expanded to include a total of 12 counties.

Geography

Guilin's world-renowned scenery is intrinsically linked to the weather. Simply put, water has carved up the landscape over several millennia. The **karst** mountains are hump-shaped because of the dissolution of their layers of soluble rock. The bedrock has been gradually washed away, leaving rocky cores that appear like mushroom stalks without their cap. The rain has also created innumerable underground drainage systems and caves, some opened to tourism, most unexplored. The abundant rivers and waterfalls are the run-off from the rainfall that has shaped this extraordinary landscape.

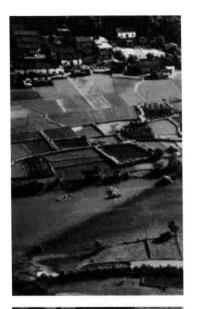

If rainwater descends directly into the subterranean environment, calcium carbonate can form in solution to drip into caves and form **stalactites** hanging from the roofs of caves and **stalagmites** building from the floor of caves. Karst caves also form twisted rock formation called **helicities** which warp in all directions, **pillars or columns** when a stalactite and stalagmites join; and **flowstones** with the build-up of calcite growth.

The weathering under karst topography can also come in a variety of forms including **bellholes** (small domes on the ceiling), **breakdowns** (rubble from falling debris), **flutes** (elongated vertical rock on the walls), **spongework** (Swiss cheese shaped holes), **pendants** (wedged or blade shaped rocks), **dripstones** (speleothems); pockets; tubes; channel in-cuts and vadose canyons.

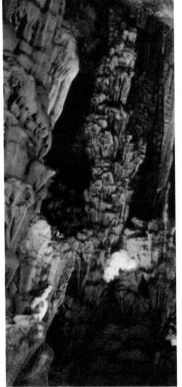

Beyond the karst, the region's topography is incredibly diverse. Near the Hunan border in **Ziyuan County** there's danxia landform – a distinctive formation found almost exclusively in South China that is created when red sandstone is compressed over millions of years. Guilin can also lay claim to the tallest mountain south of the Nanling Mountain range, the lofty **Mao'er Shan** (Cat Mountain) in **Xing'an County**, which is the source of important local rivers, the Xun and Li. The other iconic geographical image is the terraced rice paddies of Longsheng County, a stepped landscape largely created by marginalised ethnic-minority farmers forced to cultivate steep mountains.

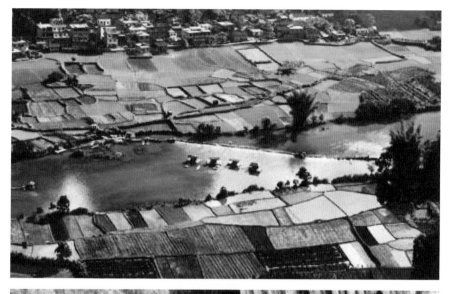

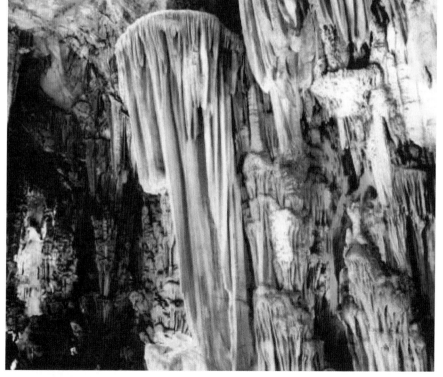

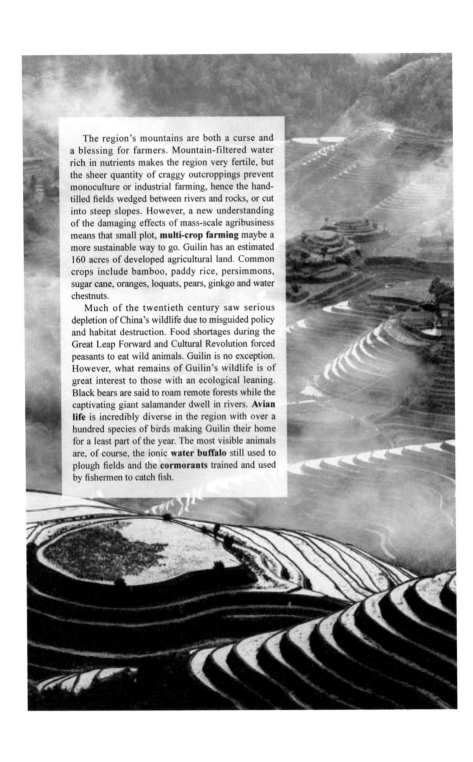

The region's mountains are both a curse and a blessing for farmers. Mountain-filtered water rich in nutrients makes the region very fertile, but the sheer quantity of craggy outcroppings prevent monoculture or industrial farming, hence the hand-tilled fields wedged between rivers and rocks, or cut into steep slopes. However, a new understanding of the damaging effects of mass-scale agribusiness means that small plot, **multi-crop farming** maybe a more sustainable way to go. Guilin has an estimated 160 acres of developed agricultural land. Common crops include bamboo, paddy rice, persimmons, sugar cane, oranges, loquats, pears, ginkgo and water chestnuts.

Much of the twentieth century saw serious depletion of China's wildlife due to misguided policy and habitat destruction. Food shortages during the Great Leap Forward and Cultural Revolution forced peasants to eat wild animals. Guilin is no exception. However, what remains of Guilin's wildlife is of great interest to those with an ecological leaning. Black bears are said to roam remote forests while the captivating giant salamander dwell in rivers. **Avian life** is incredibly diverse in the region with over a hundred species of birds making Guilin their home for a least part of the year. The most visible animals are, of course, the ionic **water buffalo** still used to plough fields and the **cormorants** trained and used by fishermen to catch fish.

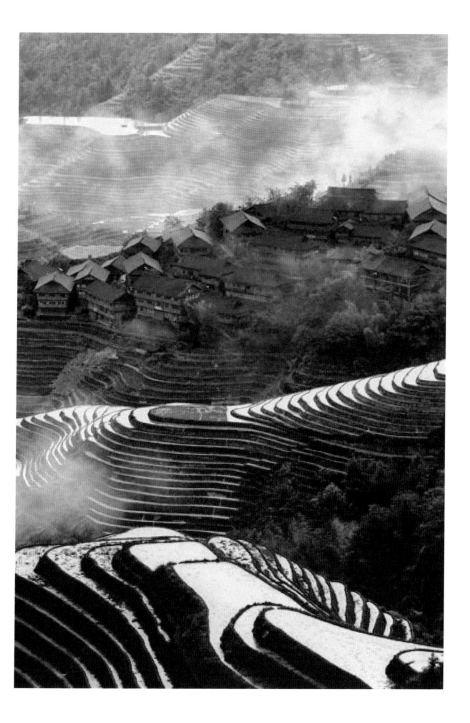

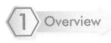

Guilin in Painting

'Guilin makes me think of the traditional Chinese paintings.'
U.S. President Bill Clinton

Our conceptions of Chinese landscape beauty are shaped by the aesthetics of the millennia old tradition of Chinese *shanshui* (mountain-river) painting, which dates back to the fifth century. The paintings have defined structural principles and typically depict landscapes using a brush and ink, rather than paints. Mountains, rivers and waterfalls are popular subjects, particularly mountains, which are sacred in Taoist culture.

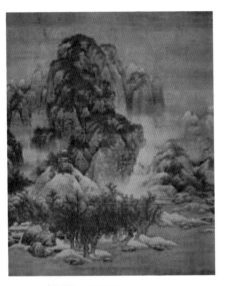

Chinese landscape painting is not naturalistic but heavily influenced by philosophical ideas. In the Tang dynasty (618-907) landscape painting embodied the literati's longing to commune with nature. In the late Tang, as order collapsed, the theme of withdrawal to the mountains became a painterly preoccupation. Meanwhile in the Mongol Yuan Dynasty (1271-1368), landscape paintings were a means of conveying the rebellious inner landscape of a Han artist's heart.

Like many apparently ancient traditions, Guilin's status as a paramount subject of Chinese landscape painting is a recent development. In the greatest age of Chinese landscape, from the Five Dynasties period to the Northern Song (907-1127), a major inspiration were the gently rolling landscapes of southeast China, where **Dong Yuan** (董源) and **Juran** (巨然) painted soft hills and rivers with rubbed brushwork. Meanwhile a rival northern school of artists like **Fan Kuan** (范宽) and **Guo Xi** (郭熙) used ink wash, stark black lines and sharp dotted brushstrokes to evoke rough-hewn northern mountains.

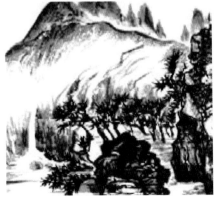

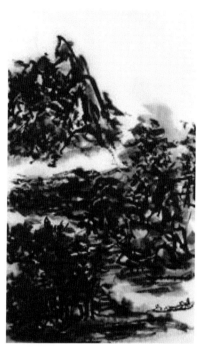

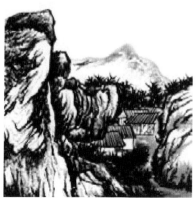

The first artist to paint the Guilin landscape is held to be **Mifu** (米芾) (1051–1107), known as the father of 'Chinese impressionism.' Mifu's used different ink shades, and large dots applied with a flat brush to render slowly flowing landscapes of rivers and clouds. His pioneering abstract style made him disliked at the Northern Song (960-1127) court. Although he was a native of Shanxi, in around 1070-1075 a 20 year old Mifu worked as a military senior official in Guilin. Many experts belief that Guilin's misty landscapes had a great influence on his artistic evolution.

The first Guilin native to swipe his ink brush across the history scroll of Chinese painting was **Shitao** (石涛), who was probably born in 1642 in the Jingjiang Prince's Palace. After his father was killed in armed rebellion in 1645, Shitao left Guilin forever. Although he is not known to have painted Guilin landscapes, his memories of home clearly influenced his works, and inspired generations of subsequent Guilin artists.

From the 18th century, an emergent Guilin art scene was dominated by three families; the **Zhou**, **Li** and **Luo**. **Zhou Weigeng** (周位庚), known as the father of Guangxi landscape painters, created a new landscape method using ocher ink ax techniques. **Li Xiyuan** (李熙垣), Zhou's son in law, followed Zhou's techniques and devoted his life to landscape painting. In 1837, a journey to Wuchang along the Li River and Xiang River inspired a 35 work River Painting series (江行图), with each creation incorporating a poem. Li Xiyuan's son **Li Jishou** (李吉寿) kept the family tradition going and their **Chongshantouo village** was renowned as a creative hotspot.

The Luo Family were equally respected for their artistic endeavours. **Luo Cunli** (罗存理) travelled widely to find creative patronage from lords and nobles. His son **Luo Chen** (罗辰), known as 'Best at painting, calligraphy and poems in Guilin' built a house on the bank of **Rong Hu** where he quickly rustled up a set of 33 paintings of Guilin scenery.

Guilin's reputation as the symbol of Chinese landscapes really hails from the first half of the

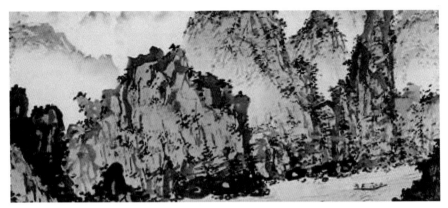

twentieth century when many prominent artists visited here. In 1905 **Qi Baishi** (齐白石) spent nearly half a year in Guilin creating masterpieces like *Solitary Beauty Peak* and *Lijiang River Rafting*. He summarized Guilin's scenery as 'peaks, banks and fishing'. Later, in 1936 another renowned master, **Xu Beihong** (徐悲鸿), came to Guilin and opened a new path in Chinese painting with his renderings of the misty rain of the Li River. Xu's innovations included giving up traditional line texturing methods for a splash ink method, and he also used clear reflections to enhance the water texture.

During China's War of Resistance Against Japan (1931-1945), waves of émigré Chinese landscape artists, fleeing from war torn regions, washed up in Guilin. As well as Xu Beihong, other greats like **Guanshanyue** (关山月), **Chang Daichien** (张大千) and **Huang Binhong** (黄宾虹) beat a path to Guangxi. Guanshanyue arrived in October 1940 and created famous landscape works such as *Li River Hundred Li* painting (漓江百里图) which portrays the whole length of the river from Guilin's Li River Bridge along to Yangshuo.

It was after this that the creative compass of Chinese landscape painting spun from the south east of China to Guilin. This development gave new impetus to local artists and encouraged the emergence of the **Li River Painting School**, whose formative figures include **Ke Tu** (涂克). Since the 1980s a group of Guangxi painters led by **Huang Gesheng** (黄格胜) have focused on the scenery of the Li River and southern Guangxi.

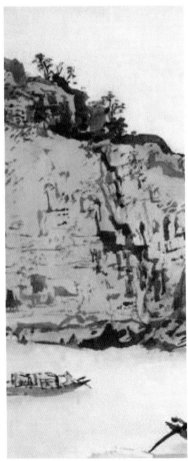

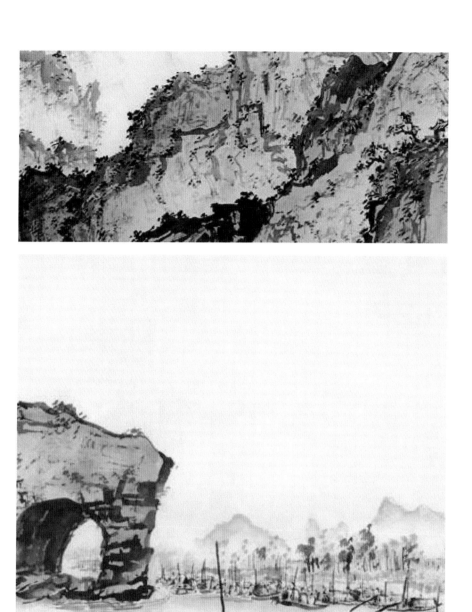

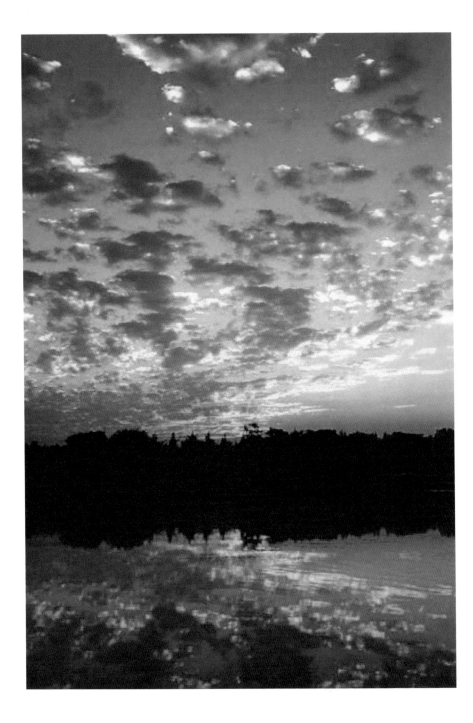

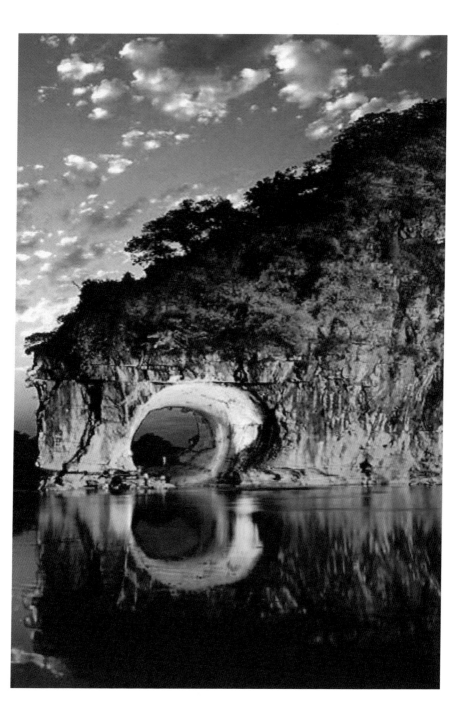

2 Guilin

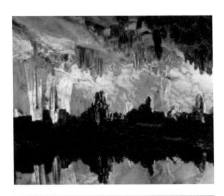

'Guilin's landscape is the best in the realm'.
Song poet Wang Zhenggong

One of China's most scenic tourist cities, osmanthus flower scented Guilin is threaded by two rivers and four lakes and studded by karst mountains.

GUILIN is situated at the start of one of the most idyllic stretches of the Li River, with **karst mountains** providing a beguiling backdrop. This beautiful city is refreshed by lakes and fragrant with the scent of **osmanthus**, the city flower. Many visitors hurry onto Yangshuo but Guilin, former seat of the **Jingjiang kings**, has enough of scenic and cultural interest to merit a longer stay.

Guilin is a comparatively low-rise city as the local government has limited the heights of buildings to 60 metres, around twenty storeys, preserving views of the karst outcroppings from almost anywhere. It is also relatively small by Chinese standards with a population hovering around the one million mark. Additionally, dispel your smoggy China stereotype; Guilin is a **protected ecological area**, where polluting industry is somewhat restricted.

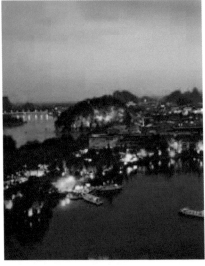

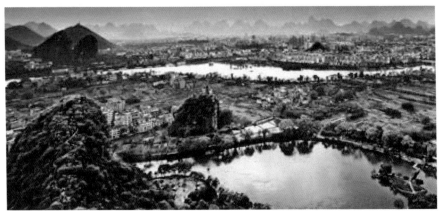

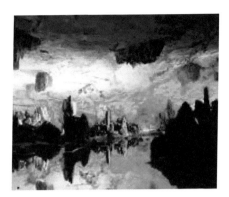

GUILIN: THE GUIDE

Guilin Sights

Many parks have been wrought from the green gold of the city's karst hills and embellished with gentle attractions. One of the most famous is **Elephant Hill**, which has become a symbol of Guilin. Many parks, particularly **Prince's City / Solitary Beauty Peak**, contain buildings of historical interest, and there are ample curiosities to uncover, from the Tang Buddhist carvings of **Xishan Park**, to the grotesque limestone formations of **Reed Flute Cave**. The peaks also offer splendid views of Guilin and the surrounding countryside.

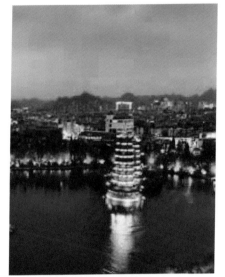

Orientation

The town centre – where most of the eating and shopping options are located, as well as several notable hotels and tourist sites – is known as the **Two Rivers and Four Lakes Scenic Area**. This district is surrounded by, and bisected with, waterways. When viewed from above, downtown looks like two urban islands connected by Guilin's major north-to-south thoroughfare **Zhongshan Road** (itself divided into Zhongshan South, Middle and North). The four lakes (*hu*) are **Sha Hu** (home of the **Twin Pagodas**) **Mulong Hu**, **Gui Hu** and **Rong Hu** while the two rivers are the **Li** and **Peach Blossom**. **Jiefang Road** crosses the scenic area's midriff connecting with **Ziyou Road** and **Seven Star Park** to the east and **Xifeng Road**, **Xishan Park** and **Guilin Museum** to the west.

Local retail outlets and brand name shops line **Zhengyang Pedestrian Street** while eateries, bars and hotels coalesce on adjoining side streets. Just east of Zhengyang, **Central Square** is (as its name suggests) a centrally located open space that more-or-

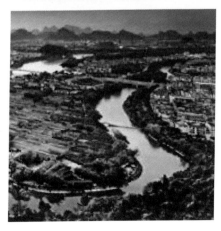

less demarks the town centre. It is a solid place to orientate your travels from (or watch the occasional public performance). Just off **Zhengyang Pedestrian Street** along **Renmin Road** you'll find the bulk of the western-friendly restaurants as well as two quality accommodation options, **Guilin Hostel** for backpackers and Sheraton **Guilin Hotel** for the executive class. Along adjacent **Binjiang Road**, which overlooks the Li River, there are also quite a few hotels, shops and restaurants to choose from. On **Zhengyanglu Xixiang**, a small lane near the **Prince's City**, you'll discover the city's religious enclave with a Catholic Church and Mosque situated side-by-side. A local entrepreneur has even opened a **Christmas Bar** next to the church. It really is Christmas every day in Guilin!

South of the **Four Lakes and Two Rivers Scenic Area** on **Zhongshan South Road**, can be found the city's old transport hub, namely the **Guilin Bus Station** and **Guilin Railway Station**. **Black Mountain Botanical Garden**, **Nanxi Park** and **Guilin Art Museum** are all located south of the centre.

Northwest of the city centre, the principle tourist attraction is **Reed Flute Cave** while the aptly named **Guilin North Station** is located quite far north of town. This brand new station takes Guilin's high-speed rail traffic. Guilin is on the Guiyang to Guangzhou HSR line.

There are several other transport hubs around the city including Chengnan Bus Station and the Beimen Bus Station. About 26 kilometres from the city centre **Liangjiang International Airport** is the region's principal airport. Amazingly, it was once known as **Kweilin Airfield** and used by the United States Army's Fourteenth Air Force, better known as the **Flying Tigers**, during World War Two. In 1991, the old airstrip was converted into a commercial airport, which now has flights to most major Chinese cities as well as several destinations elsewhere in Asia.

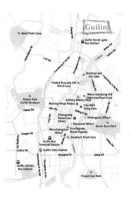

Elephant Hill Park (象山景区)

From **Elephant Hill** a trunk-like appendage snakes down to the Li River water – making it a fitting symbol for a city suckled on the river's tourism teat. The waterfront around the famous hill is a park that like many local attractions is pleasant but pricey. Inside the park a riverside path perfumed by osmanthus blossoms threads through small islands. A number of attractions have been confected, including the frankly bizarre **Mysterious Ancient Village**.

The highlight of the park is Elephant Hill itself whose intense dark foliage plunges down the slope towards the trunk. Ticket in hand you can cross the bridge from Binjiang Road and ascend to viewing platforms and the funky Ming dynasty **Samantabhadra Pagoda**, likened to a vase on the elephant's back. Carved in bluestone on the far side of the 13.6m solid brick edifice is the **Samntabadhr Boddisattva**. Behind it you will find a vertiginous spot for picture-taking.

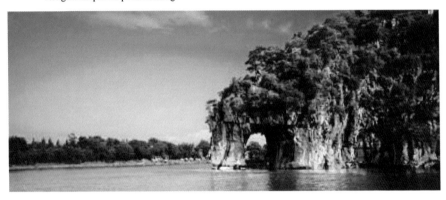

Elephant Hill Park has three entrances: Entrance One is on Minzhu Road (桂林市象山区民主路 52 号) while Entrance Two is on Binjiang Road (滨江路) and Entrance 3 is on Longzhu Road (龙珠路). Tel: 86 773 2235151. www.glxbs.com

The park is open 06.00 – 21.30 April to Oct. and 07.00 - 21.30, Nov to March. Admission is RMB75, half-price concessions.

Bus Routes: 2、16、23、33、57、58 & Tourism Bus No.1. Get off at Elephant Hill Park (象鼻山景区).

Tales of Mount Elephant (象山传奇)

A show, Tales of Mount Elephant (象山•传奇) is also held in the park. Show times are 19:00-20:00 (low season). 19:50-20:50 (peak season). Ticket price: RMB 260. Tel: 0773-2133231.

Reed Flute Cave（芦笛岩）

The "Cave for State Guests", **Reed Flute Cave** has been visited by Chinese and international leaders alike including Deng Xiaoping, Richard Nixon and George H Bush.

Situated under **Guangming Hill**, the Reed Flute Cave is also known as the "Art Palace of Nature" for its grotesque, yet beautiful limestone stalactites, stalagmites and pillars. It has taken over 180 million years for the carbon deposits to form inside the horseshoe shaped cave.

There's little need to take the rather slow **monorail** under the hill to the mouth of the cave, as it's only a 20-minute walk through the mountain park. Once entering the cool, damp cave, the rock formations have been given labelled with incredible names such as the 'Dragon Pagoda', 'Crystal Palace', 'Virgin Forest', 'Fruit Mountain', and the aptly named 'Snowman'.

When visitors reach what appears to be "frozen water", a projection of ballet dances

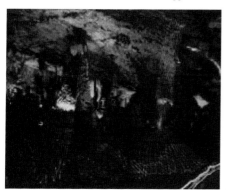 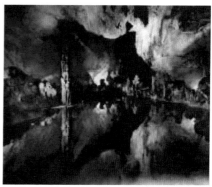

appears on the wall to the music of Tchaikovsky's Swan Lake. The Reed Flute Cave is about 240 meters wide and contains about 70 **Tang dynasty inscriptions** of travelogues and poems on its walls.

Despite the cave being visited for over 1000 years, it was only rediscovered when refugees sought refuge during the Second War of Resistance against Japan and was subsequently redeveloped and reopened in 1962 to the public. The cave's name comes from the abundant reeds that grow at the foot of the cave in **Fanglian Pond** used to make Chinese flutes.

1 Ludi Rd, Xiufeng District, Guilin（桂林秀峰区芦笛路 1 号）. www.glludiyan.com
The cave is open 06.00 to 17.30. Admission is RMB120 (monorail 35RMB).
Bus routes: 3 and 22.

Prince's City / Solitary Beauty Peak（王城／独秀峰）

A must for fans of Chinese history, this "inner-city" offers an overview of court life in imperial China, as well as an unrivalled view of the "outer-city".

Constructed in classic oblong formation, with four gates and a protective wall, the **Jingjiang Prince's Palace** was built between 1372 and 1392. It was originally intended as the official residence of a great-nephew of the first Ming dynasty emperor Zhu Yuanzhang. However, 14 Ming kings from 12 generations would come to live here.

After you pass through the majestic yellow **Chengyun Gate** you'll follow the prince's path to the **Chengyun Palace**, which is central to the whole site. It has burned down a number of times since it was originally constructed. This faithful reconstruction now houses a museum telling **the history of the Prince's City**, with limited English-language information, alas.

The **Zhuangyuan Jidi Arch** derives its name from the title awarded to someone who came first in the imperial examination. The palace was a centre for imperial recruitment during the Qing dynasty. The **Guangxi Examination Cultural Exhibition Hall**, now a museum, theatre and gift shop, was once the site where aspiring officials from all over southwest China came to sit their exams. You can even have a go yourself in one of the tiny rooms where scholars would take this infamously gruelling test. Additionally, the nearby **Fuquan Well** is said to contain blessed water, which the examinees would drink before they sat their Confucian exams.

Located at the rear of the **Prince's City**, the **Solitary Beauty Peak** is a sudden, towering karst outcropping that derives its name from the gushing prose of poet Yan Yanzi. This "Pillar under a Southern Sky" is even credited for earning Guilin its ancient slogan, "Guilin's scenery is best in the realm", from a poem by Wang Zhenggong. What the steep, 15-minute hike does offer, once you reach the pavilion at the summit, is an unrivalled panorama of the city.

Other points of interest include the **Peace Cave** where the prince worshiped, the **Reading Cave** where Yan Yanzi composed poems, and a **Sun Yat-sen monument**. The "father of the nation" stayed here while on the Northern Expedition in 1921 and even climbed **Solitary Beauty Peak**.

1 Wangcheng, Xiufeng District, Guilin, Guangxi, China（桂林市秀峰区王城路 *1* 号独秀峰•靖江王城景区内）. *Tel: 86 773 2803149. www.glwangcheng.com*

The Prince's City is open from 07.30– 18.30 (peak season) and 08.00 – 18.00 (low season). The ticket price of RMB 130 includes Solitary Beauty Peak & Jingjiang Prince's Palace .

Bus Routes: No. 1、2、9、10、11、 14、15、18、22、24. Get off at Shizijie Station（十字街站）.

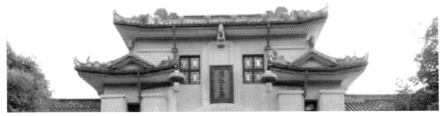

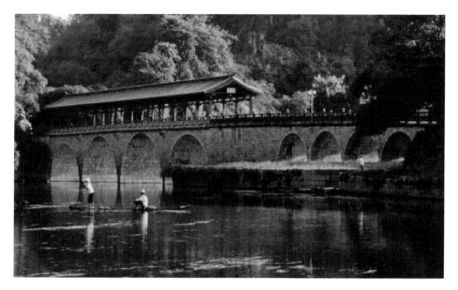

Seven Star Park（七星景区）

Situated on the eastern side of the Li River, the city's largest park derives its name from its seven mountain peaks which are said to mirror the Big Dipper constellation. It's an ancient tourist attraction established during the Sui Dynasty (681-618), and still held in high-regard (it was visited by Bill Clinton in 1998). With a modicum of gentle attractions this park is ideally suited to families with children.

As you enter you'll cross a Taoist floor motif with the animals of the Chinese zodiac and a stone lion fronting the **Flower Bridge**. This picturesque wooden-roofed stream-crossing was first built in Song Dynasty (960-1279) and earned its name from the stunning local flora.

Once you're inside you're free to roam. Many of the attractions, however, are outmoded or simply offer the opportunity for a good selfie. There are a few gentle hikes and the environment is pleasant enough, particularly around **Tianquan**

Lake. **Wild Monkeys** can be seen ambling freely about the park, accosting tourists for a free feed. The park's affiliated Seven Star Zoo is, however, not for the tender-hearted.

Highlights include **Camel Hill** – a limestone hill that looks just like a Bactrian camel and the picturesque **Qixia Temple**, which was originally built in the Tang dynasty (618-907), though it has been rebuilt and refurbished several times since. **Seven Star Cave** opens at half past each hour, when a guide leads groups around a brightly illuminated mountain chamber pointing out rocks that resemble historic characters or animals.

1 Qixing Rd, Qixing District, Guilin City（桂林市七星区七星路 1 号）. *Tel 0773-5812174.*

Opening hours are from 06.00 – 19.30 (high season), and 06.30 – 19.00 (low season). Admission costs RMB75 for the Park and RMB 60 for Seven Star Cave. A combined ticket is RMB125.

Bus Routes: No.9、10、11、14、18、21、24、25、28、30、52、97、204. Get off at Seven Star Park.

Two Rivers, Four Lakes Tour
（两江四湖）

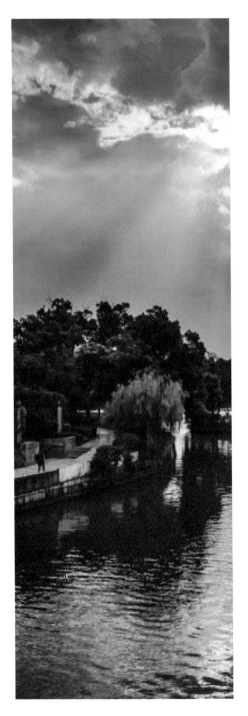

One of Guilin's top attractions is the **Two Rivers, Four Lakes** boat tour of the city waterways and lakes, best enjoyed when illuminated at night. Flotillas of tourist barges thread the **Li** and **Peach Blossom** rivers and cross four lakes, **Mulong Hu**, **Gui Hu**, **Rong Hu**, and **Sha Hu** which were formed in the Song dynasty. The formerly separate lakes were combined in 1999. In ancient times the depth of the lakes was six metres but they were drained to flood Guilin during a Song era war, and the old level never restored.

The Two Rivers, Four Lakes tour is embellished with vignettes of traditional Chinese culture. Around Mulong Hu is clustered nouveau Song dynasty architecture, including a copy of a pagoda seen in the Song era painting, *Along the River on Qing Ming Festival*. Much taxpayer gold must have been lavished on the 13 bridges along the route, which include a replica of the hump bridge from Beijing's **Summer Palace**, and the exquisite all-glass **Boli Qiao**. The biggest lake Gui Hu, originally the moat of the western Song city, is now spanned by an incongruous mock-up of the **Golden Gate Bridge**. Boats stop to observe close-up displays of **cormorant fishing**, a picturesque if cruel fishing method associated with the Li River.

The Four Lakes, Two Rivers tour perhaps aims to create something of the atmosphere of ancient China leisure craft. As boats pass, floating platforms eerily light up and troupes of performers in traditional costumes spring to life to perform numbers from the **Liu Sanjie** musical. The outwards journey culminates in a deafening Zhuang-

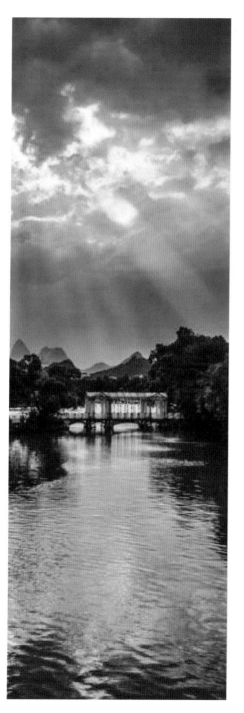

GUILIN: THE GUIDE
GUILIN: THE GUIDE

style drum performance where strobe lighting is used to blinding effect. These simulacra of traditional culture divert but evoke sadness for a lost world.

Four Rivers and Two Lakes Night Tour

1. Leaves at 19.35 from Wenchang Bridge dock & disembarks at Jiefang Bridge dock. 2. Leaves at 21.30 from Jiefang Bridge dock and disembarks at Wenchang Bridge dock. The tour takes 90 minutes, and costs RMB200/adults and RMB100/children.

Four Lakes Night Tour

Leaves from Riyuewan Dock and returns to the same dock. The 65 minute tour costs RMB190/adults and RMB95/children.

Day Tour

Leaves between 08.00 and 16.30 from Riyuewan and disembarks at Jiefang Bridge. The price for the 70 minute tour is RMB90/adults and RMB45/children.

Riyuewan Dock (日月湾码头)*: 1 Shahu North Rd, Xiangshan District, Guilin. Bus routes: take No.10、99、100 and get off at Central Square* (中心广场)*, then walk 10mins.*

Wenchang Bridge Dock (文昌桥码头)*: On Binjiang Road, take buses No. 2、16、or 23 and get off at Wenchang Bridge Station.*

Jiefang Bridge Dock (解放桥码头)*: Jiefang East Rd, Qixing District, Guilin, 桂林七星区解放东路. Take buses 10、11、or 14 and get off at Jiefang Bridge Station. Tel: 0773-2888802. www.glljsh.com/*

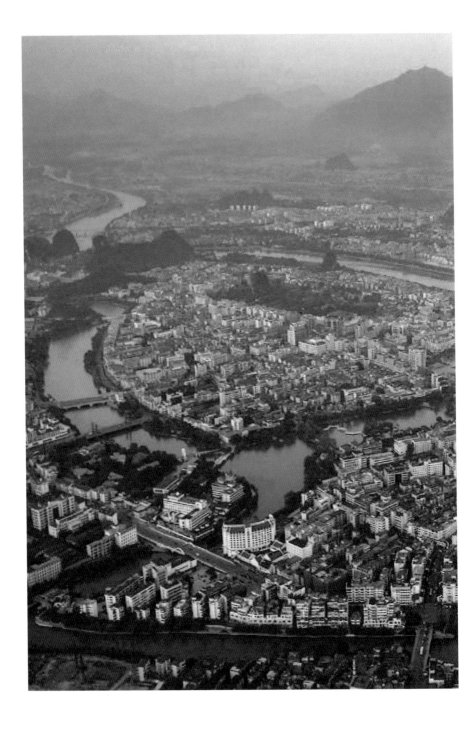

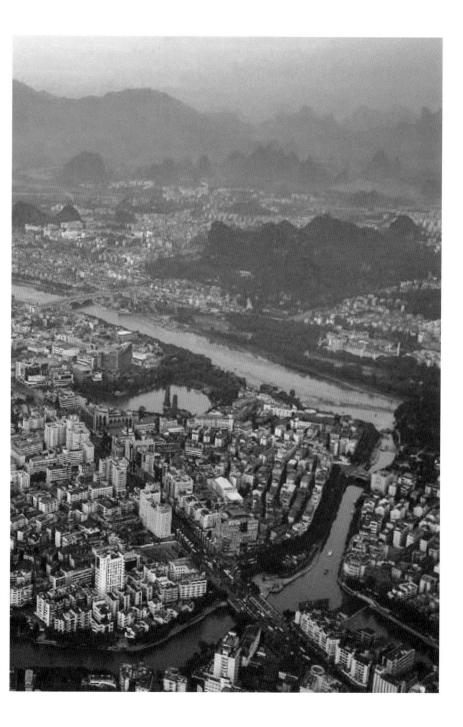

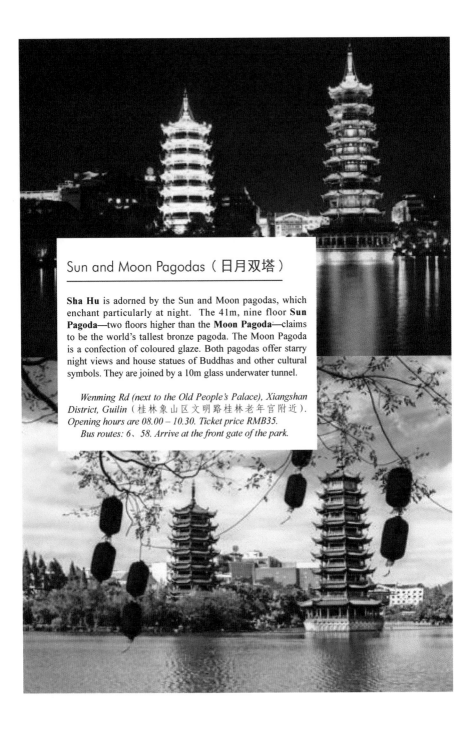

Sun and Moon Pagodas（日月双塔）

Sha Hu is adorned by the Sun and Moon pagodas, which enchant particularly at night. The 41m, nine floor **Sun Pagoda**—two floors higher than the **Moon Pagoda**—claims to be the world's tallest bronze pagoda. The Moon Pagoda is a confection of coloured glaze. Both pagodas offer starry night views and house statues of Buddhas and other cultural symbols. They are joined by a 10m glass underwater tunnel.

Wenming Rd (next to the Old People's Palace), Xiangshan District, Guilin（桂林象山区文明路桂林老年宫附近）. Opening hours are 08.00 – 10.30. Ticket price RMB35.
Bus routes: 6、58. Arrive at the front gate of the park.

The Song Gate（古南门）

Guilin's original city walls went up in the sixth year of the Han dynasty (111BC), but with the growth of the city, the walls were rebuilt during Tang times. Sadly, like many Chinese cities, presently there is precious little left of the ancient city ramparts.

The inner city walls around the **Jingjiang Prince's City** remain fairly intact but the **Ancient South Gate** is the best preserved remnant. It is one of Guilin City's outer walls and one of twelve city original gates.

A **tunnel gate** built of large, stacked, stone blocks, the Ancient South Gate is 5.3 meters high, 39.4 meters long and 19.4 meters thick. A gate was first built during the Tang dynasty, and then rebuilt during the Song dynasty, before being restored again during the Ming dynasty. The gate was repaired once more in the twentieth century and a plaque inscribed with the 'Ancient South Gate' was attached in 1963. The gate has been a popular Guilin sightseeing spot since the Qing dynasty, while today it is a popular site for couples taking wedding photos, seniors practicing tai chi and calligraphers wielding water brushes.

Northern shore of Rong Hu (Ronghu North Road), Xiufeng District, Guilin（桂林秀峰区榕湖北方岸榕湖北路）.
Admission: free.

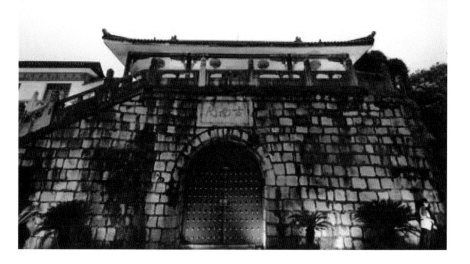

Xishan Park（西山景区）

Xishan Park's aesthetic shorthand of a pagoda on a mountain and a zigzag bridge over a lake establishes the atmosphere of a Chinese landscape painting. The two square kilometre park has three zones: **Xishan**, **Yinshan** and **Xihu** (West Lake), and a few points of historical interest. The **Tomb of Babushka**, a Soviet hero, erected in 1956, is a reminder of the close cooperation between China and Russia in the early days of the PRC. Xishan Hill is adorned with 242 modest Tang era **Buddhist carvings**, and niches and inscription from later dynasties. This was once the site of the **Xiqinglin Temple**, one of the largest Buddhist temples in South China.

2 Xishan Rd, Xiufeng District, Guilin（桂林秀峰区西山路2号）. Tel:0773-2892880.
Opening hours are 08.00 to 17.30. Ticket Prices: RMB75/adults, RMB45/children.
Bus Routes: 14、25b、89、202. Alight at the front gate.

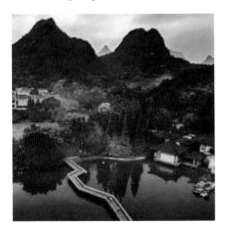

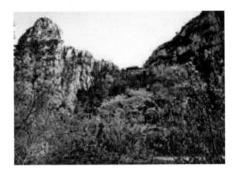

Nanxishan Scenic Area（南溪山）

Said to be one of the 'ten famous hills' of Guilin, this pretty park is centred on the two-peaked **Nanxi Mountain**. Located a little out of the town centre, Nanxi doesn't get as packed as other scenic spots. The hike itself isn't strenuous and takes you to a pavilion nestled between the two peaks from where you can enjoy a great view of the cityscape. There's also an ancient teahouse, the **Nanxi Tea House** – a Song dynasty refectory that was destroyed in World War Two, only to be rebuilt in 1985. It's a great place to enjoy the scene and "taste the spring" according to the tourist blurb. In addition, there's a ravishing **Cherry Blossom Garden** to explore as well as the decidedly less alluring **White Dragon Cave** replete with tacky illuminations. A statue in the park near Nanxi River commemorates a famous Chinese medicine prescription dating back to the Northern Song Dynasty, accredited to the immortal Liu Xianren, a character enshrouded in myth.

2 Zhongshan South Rd, Xiangshan District, Guilin（桂林市象山区中山南路二号）. Tel: 0773-381399. Open from 08:00-17.30 and tickets are RMB75.
Bus routes: 4、11、16、33、56、99. Alight at Nanxishan Park.

Guilin Museum
（桂林博物馆）

Guilin Museum's monumental facility houses China's largest collection of **plum vases**. The main exhibition however focuses on Guangxi's **ethnic minorities**. Visitors may admire a full sized model of a Zhuang stilt house, and displays of ethnic clothes and musical instruments. Life-sized human replicas in traditional costumes demonstrate **Zhuang courtship rituals** and perform the **Yao Dragon Drum Dance**. Perhaps most interesting are the legends behind these traditions, explained only in Chinese. One Yao man of antiquity, for example, is said to have fallen off a cliff while chasing a goat; the abscondent goat's skin was made into a drum and used thereafter to worship Yao ancestors. In addition to the permanent displays, there are two sizable spaces for temporary exhibitions.

Located in an alley to the west of the entrance to Xishan Park. Entrance to the museum is free but there is a charge of RMB70 – 80 for a guide. English guides are only available by prior appointment.

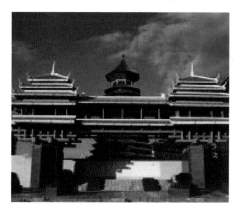

Guilin Art Museum
（桂林美术馆）

This two-storey fine art gallery is one of the largest in southwest China. Downstairs exhibitions are rotated periodically, while the second floor hosts a permanent exhibition of art works that Guilin has inspired.

It was during the creative explosion of the Song dynasty, when landscape painting came into its own, that Chinese artists began to venture into the hinterland in search of fine scenery. This trend accelerated when the Mongols established the Yuan dynasty, alienating a class of literati, who went into self-imposed exile in remote areas like Guilin.

Today, Guilin's karst landscape is intrinsically linked with Chinese landscape painting. The exhibition logically begins with mountain-water ink painting, with highlights like Ye Lumei's *Clear Evening Over the Li River* evocatively capturing the tenor of the topography.

Following on there's Chinese wood block prints such as Li Mingjiu's stunning horse and cart scene *Moving Grain* and a collection of Chinese oil paintings ranging from the impressionist to the surreal to contemporary works concerned with the effects of Guilin's modernization, notably *The One Who Yells* by Fu Junshan.

173, Longchuanping Rd, Xiangshan District, Guilin（桂林市象山区龙船坪173号 10-4）. Tel: 0773-3902889. www.glartmus. com

Opening hours are from 09.30 -16:30; the museum is closed on Monday. Admission is RMB30. Bus Routes: 4、5、11、12、 19、99、202. Get off at Nanxi Hospital.

Wave Subduing Hill（伏波山）

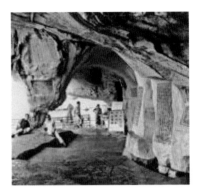

Situated on the northeast corner of the **Four Lakes, Two Rivers** area of Guilin, **Wave Subduing Hill** is one of the most accessible Guilin outcrops to reach and to climb. The hill rises to 213 metres and offers superb views of the city, the **Li River, Solitary Beauty Peak, Folded Brocade Hill** and the surrounding topography.

Before the mount stands a statue of the renowned **General Ma Yuan**, known as the "General Who Calmed the Waves". In **Pearl Returning Cave** the pillar called "**Sword Testing Rock**" is said to be have been scythed by the general, leaving the foot of the pillar with a finger-width crevice.

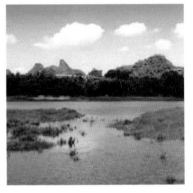

Inside the park is an enormous **cooking pot** said to be able to feed 1000 people. The pot was cast in Foshan in neighbouring Guangdong. Other attractions include a large iron bell and **Kuishui Pavilion** built in honour of General Ma Yuan on the western side of Wave Subduing Hill.

The **Returning Pearl Cave** is a labyrinth which derives its name from a local legend that a fisherman stole a 'dragon's pearl' which he later returned. At the end of the Returning Pearl Cave, the **Thousand Buddha Cave** has 239 well preserved Buddha statues and 100 inscriptions carved into the edifice of the cave during the late Tang dynasty.

26 Binjiang Rd, Xiufeng District, Guilin（桂林 秀峰区滨江路 26 号）. Tel:0773 282 5890.

Opening Hours are 07:00-18:30 daily and admission is RMB30.

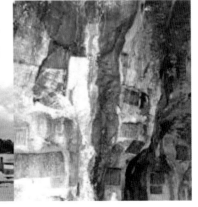

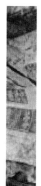

Folded Brocade Hill（叠彩山）

The quartet of peaks of Folded Brocade Hill have stunning aspects and are said to be the best vantage to take in the panoramic view. The four summits with steep stacked rocks bound with thick vegetation supposedly resemble the folds of a horse's 'brocade'.

The tallest summit of Folded Brocade Hill, **Bright Moon Peak** (223m), is a tunnel mountain, with a stout seasonal wind hole, known as the **Wind Cave** which bisects the peak. Inside the Wind Cave are about 90 bas-relief niches from the Tang and Song dynasties similar to those of **Wave Subduing Hill** but less numerous and exquisite.

The wind cave narrows to a single-file passage, with a noticeable change in temperature, and contains about 90 Buddha niches and a large Buddhist shrine, which opens on to the **Cloud Catching Pavilion**.

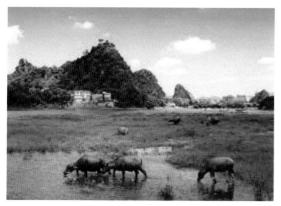

Beside the archway of the entry to the Wind Cave is a statue of noted late Qing dynasty scholar and calligrapher Kang Youwei, who famously quipped he "would rather be a *Guiliner* than a fairy". There is also a stele commemorating the Ming loyalists Qu Shisi and Zhang Tongchang.

Apart from Bright Moon Peak, Folded Brocade Hill's other peaks are **Yuyue Hill, Siwang (All-Directions-Looking) Hill, Crane Peak**, which has a precariously perched pavilion on top. The hill has a dilapidated aviary, a teahouse with tea from Yunnan, a kitsch kids slide down the mountain and a jade museum.

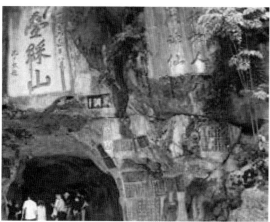

South Gate, Diecai Rd, Diecai District, Guilin（桂林叠彩区叠彩山（南门口）.

Opening Hours are 07:00-18:30 daily and admission is RMB35.

Bus routes: 2, 53 and 203.

Tunnel Hill（穿山）and Pagoda Hill（塔山）

Chuanshan or Tunnel Hill, also known as Penetrated or Pierced Hill is located to the southeast of Guilin City in **Chuanshan Park**. Facing **Elephant Hill**, Tunnel Hill overlooks the Xiaodong River (an eastern branch of the Li River).

The rugged hole that pierces Tunnel Hill is 224 meters high with the cave itself 9 meters high, 13 meters wide and 31 meters long. Legend has it that the hole was created by an arrow. At the bottom of Tunnel Hill is **Moon Cave** whose crystal or twig like outcrops are illuminated with lights.

The seven-storey '**Longevity Buddha Pagoda**' is a hexagonal Ming dynasty pagoda with Buddhist figurines which is mounted on the summit of Pagoda Hill. In the maple tree park, the irregular shape of Pagoda Hill casts a beautiful reflection of its silhouette on the waters below.

55 Chuanshan Xiaojie, Qixing District, Guilin（桂林七星区穿山小街 55 号）. *www.guilingchuanshan.com*
Opening Hours are 08:30 – 17:00 and tickets are RMB65.
Bus Route: No.6 stops at the front gate of the park.

Old Man Hill（老人山）

Old Man Hill is located in **Xiqing Lake Park** just to the north of the **Four Lakes, Two Rivers** area. The hill is said to resemble an old man with a hood, and the 'tip of the nose' has panoramic views of Guilin City including **Diecai Shan, Fubo Shan** and **Solitary Beauty Peak**.

Xiqing Lake Park, Xiqing Rd, Diecai District, Guilin（桂林叠彩区西清路西清湖）.
Free admission.

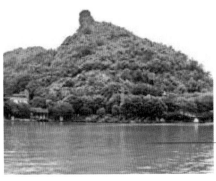

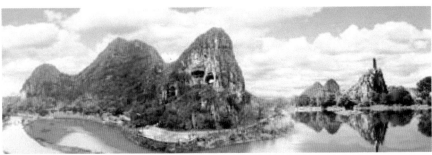

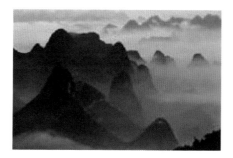

Around Guilin

Yao Mountain
（桂林尧山风景区）

Yao Mountain, situated 12km from Guilin, is the highest peak in Guilin, with an altitude of 903.3m. The name Yao Mountain comes from the **Yao Emperor Temple** which was built on its summit in Tang times. The mountain is renowned for its changing appearance. In spring Yao Mountain blossoms with Azalea, in summer it is a riot of green bamboo, in autumn it is afire with red maples, while winter carpets its slopes with snow. Besides Yao Emperor Temple, scenic spots on the mountain include **Jade Emperor Pavilion** (玉皇阁), **Tianci Field** (天赐田) and **White Deer Temple** (白鹿庵). A 1416.18m sightseeing cable car runs up the mountain.

Yao Mountain Scenic Spot, Yaoshan Rd, Diecai District,Guilin City (桂林市叠彩区尧山路尧山景区)*.*

The cable car and ropeway service operate from 09:00-16:00 but the park is open all day. Admission is RMB75 for the round-trip cable car & RMB 35 for the ropeway.

Bus route: No.24 arrives at the Yao Mountain Scenic Spot.

Gudong Waterfall
（古东瀑布）

The **Gudong Forest & Waterfall Scenic Area** is a beauty spot located 25 km to the west of Guilin City and close to the Li River in the south of **Daxu Ancient Town** of Lingchuan County. The waterfall – actually eight waterfalls and nine pools - is formed by underground streams. The elevation of the headstream is a spectacular 180m higher than that of the Li River, and visitors can actually climb one section. The waterfall scenic area consists of about 3,000 acres, including areas of subtropical & tropical rainforest. A 200m-long suspension bridge runs over the water and provides a prime position for tourists to appreciate the beauty of the Gudong forest.

Gudong Village, Daxu Town, Lingchuan County, Guilin (桂林市灵川县大圩镇古东村)*. Tel: 0773-6353081. www.glgdst.com*
Opening hours are 08.30 – 17.00. Admission is RMB80 for adults/ RMB30 children.
Take the tourist bus to Guanyan Cave from Guilin Bus Station (RMB6.5 and 40 minutes).

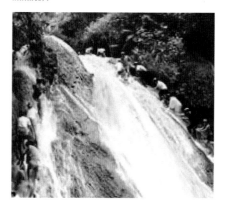

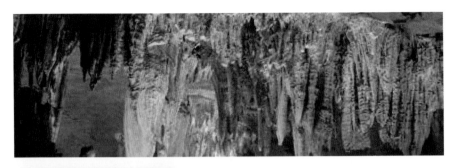

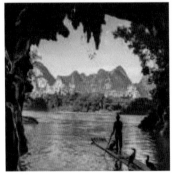

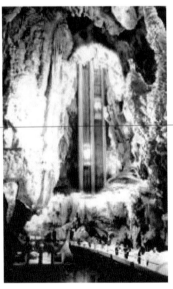

Crown Cave (冠岩)

Located 29km south of Guilin City in **Caoping Hui Nationality Village**, the Crown Cave (also known as Guanyan) is Reed Flute Cave's main rival for the title of premier Guilin 'show cave'. The cave is actually a subterranean river which flows through a hollow karst mountain into the Li River.

A tramcar takes visitors to the Li River, which is crossed by a boat to the entrance of the Crown Cave, a large hollow resembling a 'crown'. Visitors walk down into the Crown Cave to ride a flat bottomed boat along an **underground stream** through multiple separate connecting caverns.

The first two caverns are dry karst with **spectacular stalactites**, stalagmites and stone pillars and outcrops in colossal vaults. The third chamber is a **subterranean river** which flows directly into the Li River. The sweet green water crashing at high pressure through the Crown Cave sprays a purple mist. There is also a waterfall (requires a separate ticket).

The Crown Cave actually has about 12km of passage ways, although only three kilometres of cave are accessible to the public. There are **multiple routes** to explore the cave. An eclectic mix of transport systems includes a toboggan like roller coast rail car, boats, and Asia's first **cave elevator**, which you can ride back up to the surface.

Guanyan Scenic Resort, Caoping Town, Yanshan Distict, Guilin (桂林雁山区草坪乡). Tel: 0773-3858131. www.liriver.org

Opening hours are 08.00 – 16.30. Tickets are RMB80. Buses leave for Crown Cave from Guilin and Yangshuo, and some cruise ships also dock there.

Guilin Tea Science and Research Institute
（桂林茶叶科学研究所茶叶科技园）

This out-of-town locale is a real hidden gem and a must for tea fiends. Located on the site of a Ming-era tea garden, next to **Yao Mountain**, the city' highest, this government-operated facility was established in 1965 to investigate the science behind the many medicinal benefits of tea consumption, as well as developing the means of tea cultivation. The site currently covers 40 bucolic hectares containing 250 tea plants. The institute keeps a further 300 kinds of tea genes and boasts the first **organic tea garden** in the province. There are currently 37 sciences working at the institute.

The institute also offers guided tours for visitors. The tour begins when a guide takes you to the tea fields to explain how different teas are cultivated. You can even have a go picking some of the good leaf yourself. Next, there's an exhibit of the traditional tools used to turn the fresh leaf into fine dried tea ready for drinking. The visitation is rounded up with a **Tang dynasty tea ceremony**, during which your guide will show you the etiquette integral to the Tao or "way" of tea, before leaving you free to roam the teashop, where the high-grade produce of the institute (most of which is unavailable on the open market) is for sale.

17 Jinji Rd, High-tech Development Zone, Qixing District, Guilin（桂林七星区高新开发区金鸡路 *17* 号查课所内）. *Tel:0773-5600981.*

Opening hours are 9:00-17:00. Free admission. English speaking guides may be booked in advance.

On The Guilin Tea Trail
（桂林茶）

Chinese tea is most readily associated with the provinces of Yunnan, Guangdong, Fujian, Hunan, Zhejiang and Jiangsu. Poor old Guangxi is criminally overlooked. Guilin in particular, with its protected environment and unique terroir, has some fine teas to speak of. The most famous is **guihua**（桂花茶）or **osmanthus flower tea**. The city's name Guilin literally translates as "osmanthus forest" and the sweet tea made with the city's favourite flower is said to be helpful for weight loss, not to mention popular with the ladies. Cat Mountain is where quite a lot of local tea is produced, including rare **yellow tea** made from short plants and tiny leaves, which is good for cleansing one's kidneys. Cat Mountain's wild tea is also being processed and sold. The sumptuous black tea **Lao Shan Jie Liu Dong Cha**（老山界六垌茶）and sweet green leaf **High Mountain Tea**（野生甘露茶）are available from select pioneering vendors. Traditional, manual, tea producing techniques are still prevalent throughout the region and if you don't get to **Guilin Science and Tea Research Institute** for a comprehensive overview, opposite **Camel Hill** in **Seven Star Park**, you can pick-up some hand prepared, fried, fresh tea.

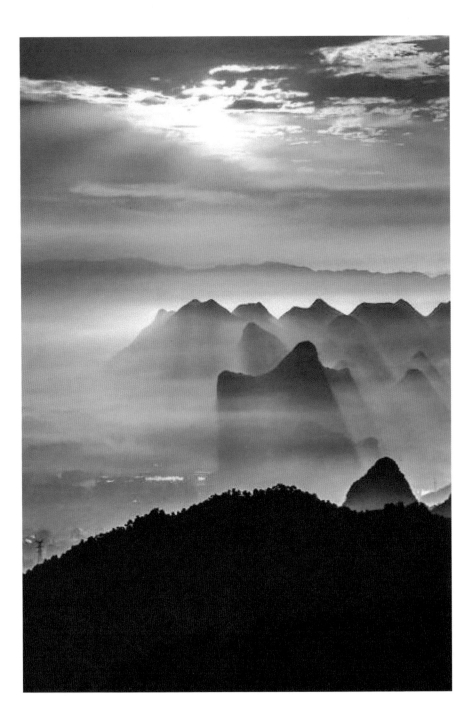

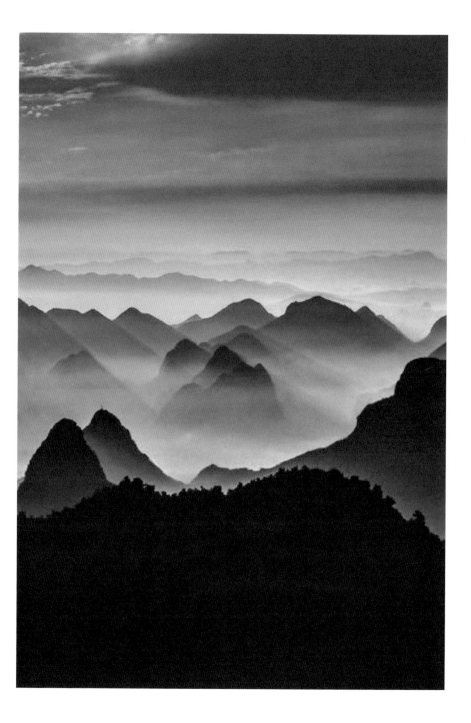

3 Dragon's Backbone Rice Terraces

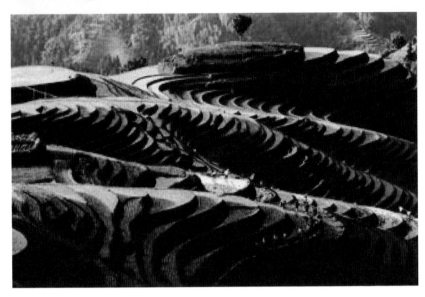

*It is the terraced fields that have earned this county its illustrative name, which means literally **Dragon's Backbone**. When the paddy fields fill with water in the spring, they glitter in the sunlight, giving an ethereal quality to the spectacular scene.*

BEFORE the tarmac arrived at the turn of the millennium, the **Dragon's Backbone (Longji) Rice Terraces** were a mysterious place, known to but a few hearty travellers. At the highest reaches around **Tiantou Village** (田头寨) there was no electricity. The local Yao and Zhuang minority people lived a secluded life, away from the fray of boom-time China.

This is no longer the case. Things change fast in China and in the decade and a half since the region was "opened-up", restaurants and hotels, as well as amenities like car parks, bus stops and a cable car, have turned this once isolated area into one of the Southwest's most venerable tourist attractions. So what is bringing tourists in their busloads to this remote quarter of Guilin?

Quite simply, it's the marvel of the rice terraces. Unlike the karst landscape synonymous with Yangshuo, which was carved by mother nature, the iconic terraced hills of Longsheng County were very much made by the hand of man. Over six hundred years ago ethnic minority groups, in particular the Yao, fleeing Han Chinese encroachment, were pushed higher and higher into the hills. Forced to cultivate ever-steeper slopes, they cut the landscape into the remarkable step formations that remains to this day.

However, it should be noted that while tourism has made hoteliers out of subsistence farmers, the influx of the outside world has eroded the cultural distinctiveness of Longji. The pollution that accompanies mass tourism is particularly prevalent in peak seasons. And at the time of writing, a second road under construction is likely to deliver even more holidaymakers to Longji, so plan your visit carefully!

Longsheng Overview and Orientation

Located 100km to the northwest of Guilin City the riverside town of **Longsheng** is a vibrant little place. It's had a makeover in recent years, repainted and illuminated at night and there are plenty of eateries and places to stay.

However, it is not the main attraction, merely an administrative centre and jumping-off station from where one can explore the wonders of the surrounding countryside. There are famous mountains, ethnic minority villages, waterfalls and Communist "red" history sites to discover in all directions. But of particular note, to the northeast you'll find a road leading past the **Forest Park** to the **Longsheng Hot Springs**,while to the southeast, just past Heping Village, the **Longji Terraced Scenic Area** is undoubtedly the county's principal attraction.

If you're not on an all-inclusive **Longsheng** tour from Guilin, you'll probably have to change bus at **Longsheng Bus Station**. This busy station also has buses for nearby counties like **Ziyuan** as well as long distance services to **Shenzhen** and **Guangzhou**. From whichever locale you set out for Longsheng you'll need to decide whether to begin your hike in **Longji**, **Ping'an** or **Dazhai**.

Private car / mini-van hire is an option and available from various points in Longsheng / Longji, as well as to and from Guilin. Prices range between RMB50 – 100 per person, depending on the season and whether or not you can fill the vehicle.

Longsheng – Guilin
Between 06:30 and 19:00, every half an hour (RMB28).
Ping'an – Longsheng
07:30, 9.00 11:00, 13:00, 15:00, 17:00. (RMB8).
Longsheng– Ping'an
07:40, 9:20, 11:00, 13:00, 15:00, 17:00. (RMB8).
Dazhai– Longsheng
Between 08:30 and 17:30, every hour. (RMB9).

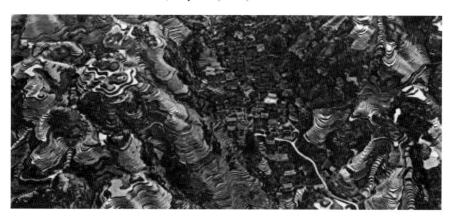

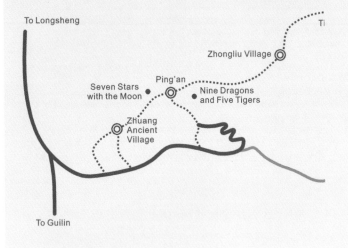

To Longsheng

Music From Paradise

Ti

Zhongliu Village ◎

Ping'an

Seven Stars
with the Moon ●   ◎   ● Nine Dragons
                        and Five Tigers

◎ Zhuang
Ancient
Village

To Guilin

Longji Terraces Scenic Area（龙脊风景区）

At the entrance to the **Longji Terraces Scenic Area** there's an entrance ticket where your bus / car will stop for you to buy a mandatory **RMB100** ticket. After this there remains a considerable drive into the scenic area itself, which is home to 13 villages in total. The first village is **Jinzhu** (金 竹), a Zhuang village where the film *Passion of Buluotuo River* and TV series *Brave as a Lion* were both filmed. From there, you'll come upon a number of Yao and Zhuang villages lining the road. All have ethnic handicraft stalls as well as family run guesthouses and rural family restaurants. If you've hired a private vehicle it can be worth stopping for a riverside lunch en route to the terraces.

Golden Buddha
Peak

9 ●

Tiantou Dazai   Xiaozai
        Village   Village

Jinkeng Red
Yao Terraced
Fields

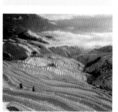

Hiking

The tried and tested hike route is along the old stone trail that connects the principal villages of the **Longji Scenic Area**. They are the **Longji Zhuang Ancient Village** (龙脊古壮寨), **Ping'an** (平安寨), **Zhongliu Village** (中六村), **Tiantou** (田头寨), **Dazai Village** (大寨) and **Xiaozai Village** (小寨).

Most visitors enter by vehicle into the scenic area and head directly to the highest ticket examination office at **Dazhai**. This will gain them access to the Yao villages of **Xiaozhai, Xinzhai** and **Tiantou**. There is a cable car here as well as some of the best small hikes. The many famous scenic spots include **Golden Buddha Peak** (金佛顶), and **Music From Paradise** (西山韶乐).

Then, after a good night's sleep in a local hotel (there are plenty to choose from in **Tiantou** and around), begin the hike downhill through the other villages taking in the bucolic scenery en route.

Around **Ping'an**, you can enjoy two notable viewpoints, the **Nine Dragons and Five Tigers** (九龙五虎) and **Seven Stars with the Moon** (七星伴月), whereas the **Longji Zhuang Ancient Village** boasts **The First Rice Terrace** (始祖田), **Slender Ditch** (长沟) and **Floating Dragons to the River** (游龙下江) view points.

There's a ticket examination office, car park and bus stop at **Ping'an** and **Longji Zhuang Ancient Village** as well as **Dazhai**. Conversely some decide to start at the bottom, or midway and hike upwards. Either way you should consider giving yourself seven to eight hours if you're not in a hurry. Some even do the hike in two stages, stopping half way to stay overnight in one of the villages before moving onwards.

You should also think about hiring a local guide. Just ask around in the villages, the going rate is RMB100-150 per day (plus lunch). For off-the-beaten path rambles a guide is more or less essential, as this region has few safety provisions to speak of.

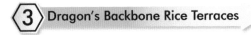

Longji Ancient Zhuang Village
(龙脊古壮寨)

This village is unmissable for those who are interested in history and culture.

The village boasts some of the oldest and the largest stilted buildings in the province, most of which are more than 100 years old. The village itself has a history of over 400 years.

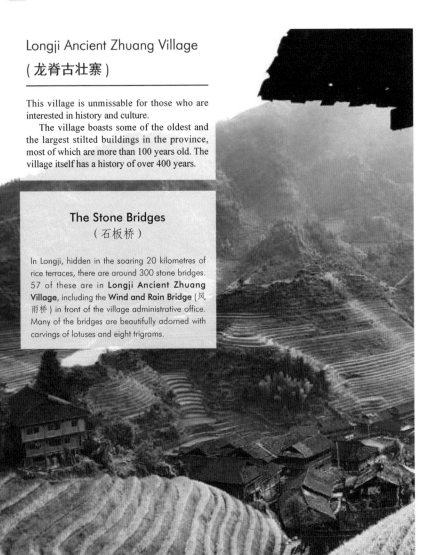

The Stone Bridges
(石板桥)

In Longji, hidden in the soaring 20 kilometres of rice terraces, there are around 300 stone bridges. 57 of these are in **Longji Ancient Zhuang Village**, including the **Wind and Rain Bridge** (风雨桥) in front of the village administrative office. Many of the bridges are beautifully adorned with carvings of lotuses and eight trigrams.

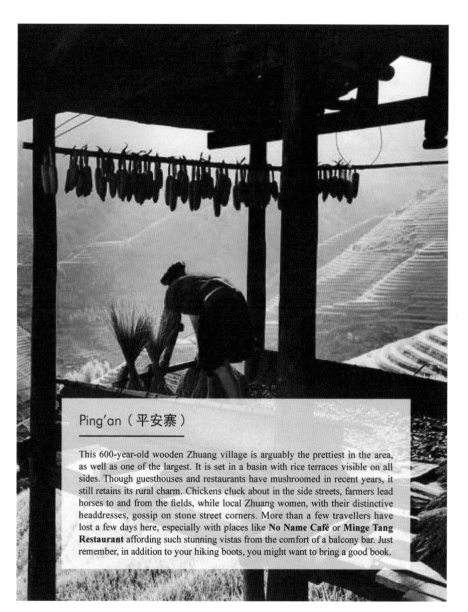

Ping'an（平安寨）

This 600-year-old wooden Zhuang village is arguably the prettiest in the area, as well as one of the largest. It is set in a basin with rice terraces visible on all sides. Though guesthouses and restaurants have mushroomed in recent years, it still retains its rural charm. Chickens cluck about in the side streets, farmers lead horses to and from the fields, while local Zhuang women, with their distinctive headdresses, gossip on stone street corners. More than a few travellers have lost a few days here, especially with places like **No Name Café** or **Minge Tang Restaurant** affording such stunning vistas from the comfort of a balcony bar. Just remember, in addition to your hiking boots, you might want to bring a good book.

Jinkeng Red Yao Terraced Fields（金坑红瑶梯田）

1000 metres above sea level, the lands at the top of the **Longji Scenic Area** belong to the Red Yao. There are several villages clinging to the hills among the clouds. **Dazhai** (literally Big Village) has the ticket examination office, bus station and car park. The cable car also begins here with an additional cost of RMB120 / 70, double or single way. There are some pleasant restaurants and guesthouses including **Yuan Meng Ju** and **Da Ji Yao Zhai International Youth Hostel**.

Tiantou, meaning Field Head, is the highest village, located half way up **West Hill Music Scenic Spot**（西山韶乐）, which, at 1, 100 metres, is the highest point in the area for that must-get selfie. Traditional wooden houses here cling to the mountainside offering unrivalled views of the stepped paddies. The local Yao folk are all surnamed Pai. The women in particular are busy sewing and hawking traditional textiles, or letting down their uncut hair, usually for a fee.

Plenty of **Tiantou** farmers have converted their three-storey, traditional wooden homes into guesthouses and there are two **YHA youth hostels** up there as well, notably **Dragon's Den Hostel**. Other villages include **Xinzhai**, **Xiaozhai** and **Zhongliu**, the latter of which is situated half way down the path between **Ping'an** and **Tiantou** and boasts a few earthy eateries and guesthouses of its own.

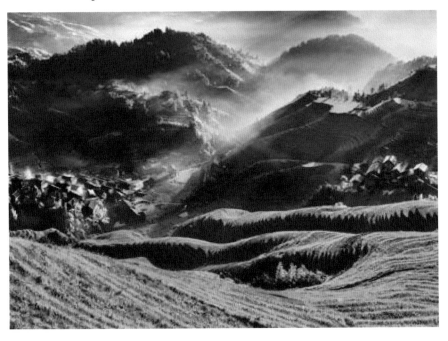

Longsheng Hot Springs（龙胜温泉）

The thermal activity beneath craggy Guilin has led to the establishment of several hot spring resorts scattered around the county. They are of variable quality. By far and away your best bet in terms of cleanliness and all round quality can be found in the **Longsheng Hot Spring Tourist Area**.

After hiking the rice terraces, this is a conveniently located retreat to kick back and nurture those aching muscles. To get there take the road heading northeast out of **Longsheng Town** towards **Ziyuan County**（资源县）. The hot springs resort is 32km away from the town. En route, you'll pass through several ethnic minority villages with rural family restaurants serving up local fare. There's a stunning **Forest Park**（森林公园）if you've the energy for more hikes and scenic spots, situated just ahead of the entrance to the resort area.

Comprising three hotels, this riverside pleasure palace boasts a stunning forested mountain backdrop from which the naturally heated mountain water excretes at a natural temperature of 50 degrees centigrade. There are several soothing pools of varying temperatures to hop in, and according to the blurb, the water here contains at least ten trace elements that are beneficial to humans. There's also a spring water swimming pool, kissing fish lagoon and spa. The basic cost per person is RMB128, though select facilities require an additional fee. Swimming trunks can be purchased near the entrance if you've neglected to pack a pair.

Ailing Hot Spring Zone, Longsheng County, Guilin（桂林市龙胜县矮岭温泉区）.
Tel:0773-7482888. www.ls-wq.com

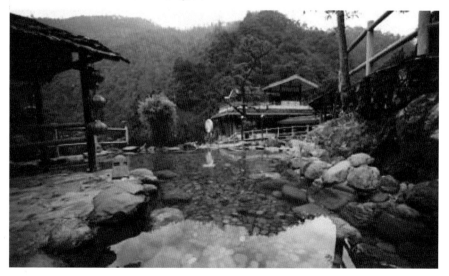

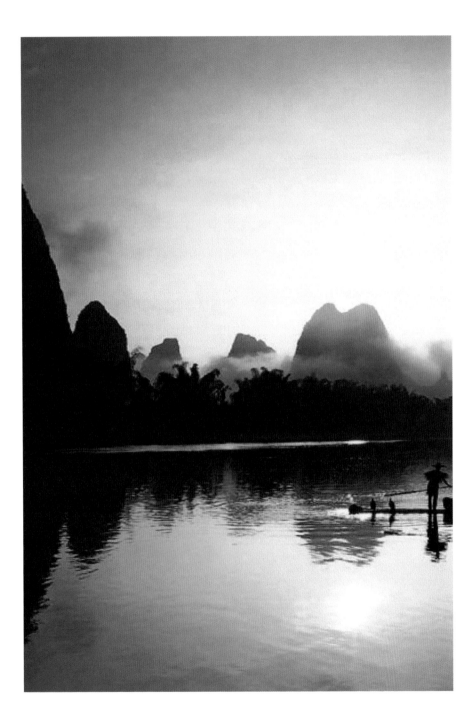

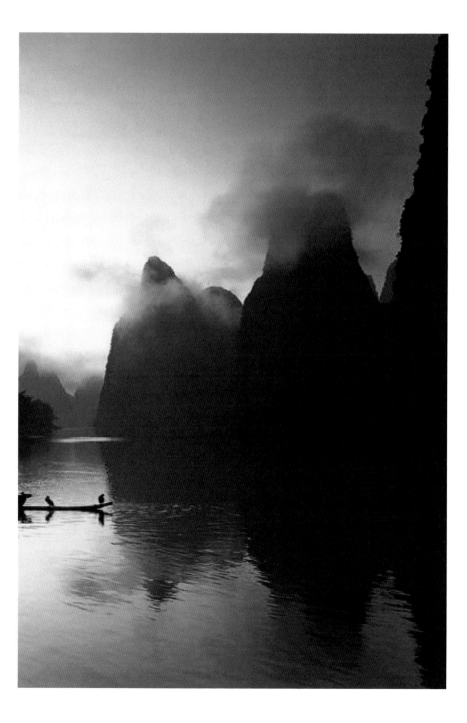

4 The Li River

'The river forms a green gauze belt, the mountains are like jade hairpins'.
Han Yu, a Tang Dynasty poet

Overview

The Li River is the Guilin centrepiece, synonymous with the bucolic scenery it has both sculpted and fed for eons. Some part of its winding jade waters, flanked by lurching karst mountains, will be included in any given Yangshuo postcard.

THE Li River is part of an historic system of waterways connecting the **Yangtze River** in central China with the **Pearl River Delta** in southern Guangdong. The river originates in **Cat Mountain** (you can visit the swampy source) in Xing'an County to the north of Guilin. Upstream, the Li River is linked by the **Lingqu Canal** with the **Xiang River**, which flows north into the mighty Yangtze. The Lingqu Canal, built by China's first emperor Qin Shihuang, is one of the oldest human-made waterways in the world. This explains why many ancient towns like **Daxu** have evolved along its banks. They were market towns on edge of an ancient highway system.

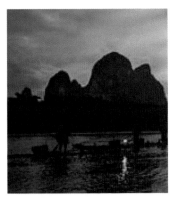

The generally shallow and sometimes steep sided Li River flows through villages and bamboo forests with karst formations all around. In **Pingle**, the river merges with the Lipu and **Gongcheng** Rivers and continues south as the **Gui River**, which at Wuzhou eventually flows into the **Xi River**, the western tributary of the Pearl River.

The water may appear clean but the sharp rise in tourism-associated emissions presents an environmental challenge. More two million Guilin locals earn their living from the river. With this income stream difficult to resist, it will be necessary to raise local people's environmental consciousness if the Li River tourism is to be sustainable.

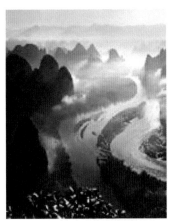

Landscape

The combined length of the Li and Gui Rivers is 437km but the most acclaimed scenery is found between Guilin

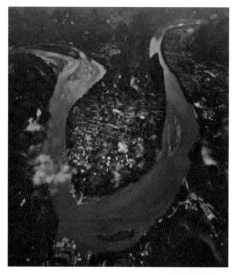

and Yangshuo, and in particular the span between **Yangdi** and **Xingping**.

Millions each year take to the Li River's green waters in tourist boats and bamboo rafts, weaving between analogic peaks, submerged islands, and paddy fields, in search of scenery that has come to epitomize Chinese landscape beauty. As the river meanders south towards Yangshuo the karst formations become more picturesque, with many having names like **Camels Crossing the River** and **Nine Horses Picture Hill.** At Xingping is the **Yellow Cloth Shoal** landscape memorialized on the fifth series of the 20 yuan note. The landscapes can be enjoyed in any weather, but wrap up well in winter.

Exploring the River

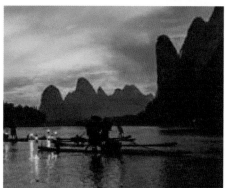

The classic way to enjoy the river scenery is to join the crowds on tourist boats from Guilin to **Yangshuo.** Boats come with talkative guides who introduce the scenery along the route and the journey takes four to five hours to reach the Yangshuo ferry.

Another option is to embark from Yangdi, a one hour (if lucky) drive from Guilin. From Yangdi, **motorised bamboo rafts** can be chartered to the Nine Horse Picture Hill, or beyond to Xingping. This is a more intimate way to imbibe the river's presence.

Perhaps a better choice though is to **hike** a stretch of the river, soaking up the immensity of the landscape and the charm of the villages and rural scenes. Regulations about hiking the river are fluid and many travellers end up making the journey by a combination of hike and motorised transport.

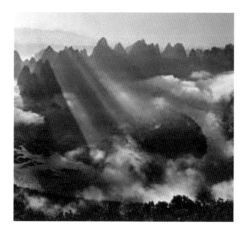

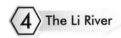

Cruise Boat from Guilin to Yangshuo

From Guilin, tourist barges bear battalions of amateur photographers down the river towards Yangshuo. The four-to-five-hour trip could possibly seem longer as garrulous guides describe the river sights.

Boats with Chinese speaking guides embark from **Mopanshan Pier**, a 40 minute drive from downtown Guilin. Tickets can be scored at Guilin travel agents and hotels for RMB245-260, including a free shuttle bus, which picks up from various places around town. Alternatively make your way to the pier by taxi for about RMB100 and buy tickets there for RMB210.

The higher priced boats with English-speaking guides leave daily at 10am from **Zhujiang Pier**, fifteen minutes upstream from Mopanshan, which Zhujiang vessels pass on the way down. As with the Chinese boats, tickets can be bought all around town, and the cost is around RMB420, again including a shuttle bus to the pier.

Once the boats get underway, passengers admire the passing scene from eight-seater tables in the lower deck cabin while a basic lunch is served. The best views, however, are from within the maelstrom of photo-takers on the upper deck. It is possible to pay an extra 50 yuan to sit in one of the upper-deck private, railway style compartments, although in practice these seats seem hard to score.

Some of the best scenery of the cruise comes just before the Nine-Horse Picture Hill when a bend in the river opens broad vistas. A range of hills run across the horizon, resplendently green and embroidered with saddle-like twin peaks. Besides these hills, the exposed white limestone of the Nine-Horse Picture Hill presents a satisfying contrast.

The boats come to a rest at **Yangshuo Ferry** where alighting passengers run a course of tourist tat vendors and bee keepers touting local honey. Note that the tourist boats only run services with the flow of the river from Guilin to Yangshuo, which is why you will see them returning empty from Yangshuo to Guilin.

Mopanshan pier. Guimo Rd, Lingchuan County, Guilin, （磨盘山码头，桂林灵川县桂磨路尽头）.

Zhujiang pier. 91 County Road, Yanshan District, Guilin, （竹江码头，桂林雁山区091县道）.

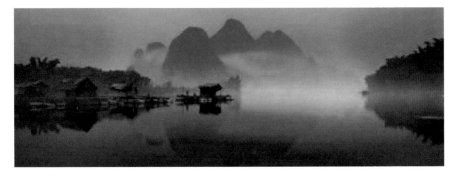

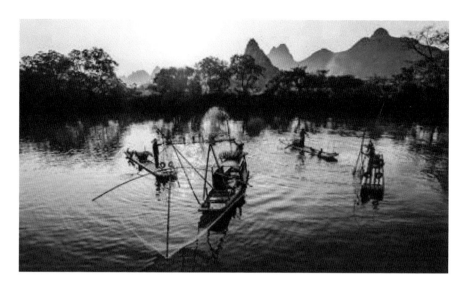

Motorised Bamboo Rafts

Yangdi Ferry (see page 74), one hour from Guilin, is the place to embark on more intimate explorations of the Li River between Yangdi and Xingping, either by foot or motorized bamboo raft. From the smaller bamboo rafts, there are better views of sights such as the Nine Horse Picture Hill (some of the horses are low down).

Boat tickets can be had from the tourist information centre located in a big concrete hall behind the square where the Guilin buses stop. The boats, made out of faux-bamboo and powered by two-stroke outboards, line up on the river. Most take four passengers so if you lack a quorum, you will have to pay an empty seat supplement (about 25 yuan).

The flotilla of boats can seem chaotic in peak season, and be prepared to sprayed from the wake of other boats; however, there are canopies to protect from wind, rain and sun, and passengers wear yellow life jackets. If someone in your party understands Chinese, the boat captain will explain the sights en route and slow down to allow photographs.

Forty minutes later, boats tether beneath the **Nine Horse Picture Hill** and passengers climb a bank to a carpark where *dianche* (glorified golf buggies) wait for the onwards journey to Xingping. In winter, if traffic is slow, these may take as few as two people for no surcharge. The road heads through pretty cultivated land, then bears back towards the river near **Yellow Cloth Shoal** (the 20 yuan note scene). You will know when this is close because the banks bustle with tourist stalls and people. Disembark at Yellow Cloth Shoal to enjoy or photograph the view, and then walk the 10-15 minutes to Xingping. Otherwise if you choose to stay in the *dianche*, it will drop you near **Xingping Bus Station**.

Tickets for the 40 minute ride to Nine Horse Picture Hill cost about RMB120, which includes free onwards travel to Xingping by dianche *(15 minutes). If you choose to walk on to Xingping, which takes three hours, the cost is the same. On the other hand, it only costs RMB30 more to boat it all the way to Xingping.*

68

Scenic Highlights Along the Li River

The Li Fish（鲤鱼挂壁）

Low on a cliff near the first bend of the river past the Yangdi ferry leaps a large stone fish – the Li Fish. The fish with its reddish hue may not be visible from the big tourist barges but the smaller crafts will cast their line close to it.

Divine Pen Peak
（神笔峰）

An outcrop suggestive of an ink pen juts out from verdant green on the west bank of the river.

An Old Person Guards
An Apple（老人守苹果）

This perfectly round peak has a small concave dip on top – very much like the Apple logo. Beside the 'apple', a proturbance resembling an old person is keeping guard of it.

Camels（骆驼过江）

At this spot a line of camels appears to be passing the river.

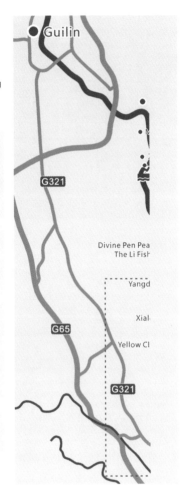

Guilin

G321

Divine Pen Pea
The Li Fish

Yangd

Xial

Yellow Cl

G321

G65

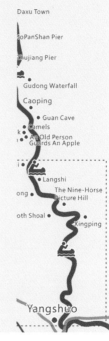

Daxu Town

PanShan Pier

Zhujiang Pier

Gudong Waterfall

Caoping

Guan Cave

Camels

An Old Person
Guards An Apple

Langshi

The Nine-Horse
Picture Hill

oth Shoal

Xingping

Yangshuo

The Nine-Horse Picture Hill
（九马画山）

This 100 meter high cliff, thanks to a combination of weathering and rock strata, supposedly resembles a painting of nine horses. Tour guides challenge their captive audiences to identify the nine. The snorting steed at the top is easily harnessed but some others demand giving free rein to your imagination. In case of discouragement, take heart from the apocryphal tale that saintly former Premier Zhou Enlai easily identified the nine.

Yellow Cloth Shoal (The 20 Yuan Note)（黄布倒影）

The Yellow Cloth Shoal scenery, which features on the back of the RMB20 note, is seen just round the big turn that the river takes at Xingping. The banknote shows a cormorant fisherman on the river with Yellow Cloth Shoal behind it. The shoal's name comes from a maize-yellow flagstone, long and wide, whose reflection spreads itself on the river, like a yellow cloth.

The seven hills on the bank of Yellow Cloth have been likened to seven fairy maidens who came from heaven to play at the bank and were so amazed by the scenery they wouldn't leave. The Emperor of Heaven ordered them back and the fairies changed themselves into hills in order to stay.

Yellow Cloth Shoal is known locally as the best place to see reflections in the water. The refections vary with the weather, broken by drops of rain on wet days, limpid and clear under sun. The best angle to see the reflection is when the boat turns at the Mahuang Sandbar and the inverted peaks float in the water with shadows around.

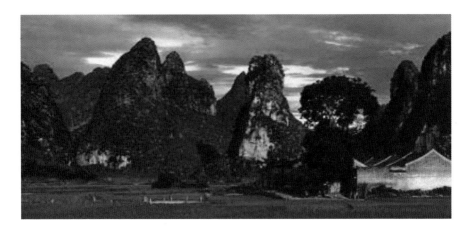

Hiking

Hiking from Yangdi to Xingping is often considered the best way to fully appreciate the splendid **Li River scenery**. The usual hike takes in six countryside fishing villages and numerous karst peaks, bamboo groves, orchards and paddy fields, and involves making **three river crossings**. However, the route is currently mired in uncertainty.

In 2012, the government introduced a RMB180 charge for the hike, which included the three ferry crossings. In the winter of 2015, the government **stopped sale** of the tickets, claiming 'safety' issues. Because it is necessary to cross the river three times, it has become a challenge to complete the hike independently. For now, it is usually necessary to get a bamboo boat to Nine Horse Picture Hill and then hike from there, which misses out the best part of the route.

The word is that the government does plan to open the hiking route again in 2016 and is currently upgrading the path from Yangdi to Xingping. It remains to see how the hike will change after this upgrade.

Assuming the route is the same, after buying tickets, the hike starts with a short boat ride from Yangdi Ferry to the far bank. There the sometimes muddy path runs towards the beguiling **Langshi** (wave rock) **Village** (浪石村) where wait vendors of sweet potatoes, corn, noodles, water, and raincoats. At Langshi, cross the river again to **Quanjiazhou** (全家洲) and walk for a while on the other side. From Quanjiazhou, most hikers walk on to **Lengshui** (冷水) before crossing the river again to **Xialong** (下龙).

After the Nine Horse Picture Hill the route to Xingping runs inland across a picturesque landscape of cultivated land between hills. It is not really possible to get lost because there is only one path; however, some hikers have complained that the crossings are not well signposted, making it easy (especially under pressure from bamboo boat touts) to cross in the wrong place.

The hike from Yangdi to Xingping has been estimated at 18-25km and it takes anything from 4.5-6 hours. The first stage from Yangdi to Nine Horse Fresco Hill or 'Jiumahua' (九马画) is about 10m. Allow around 3 hours for the 14km section from Nine Horse Picture Hill to Xingping.

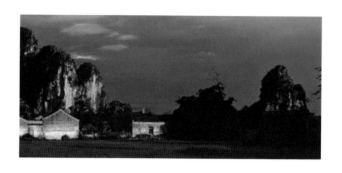

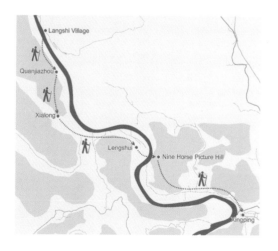

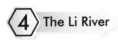

Ancient River Towns

Daxu Ancient Town
(大圩古镇)

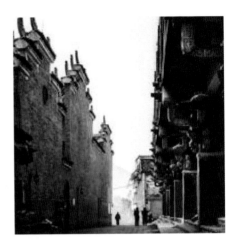

Daxu Ancient Town is a real treasure for history buffs and its location, just 20 kilometres southeast of Guilin, makes it well worthy of a day trip from the city. Daxu literally means Big Market and this place really does have a long mercantile history to speak of. Founded in the Qin Dynasty, 2000 years ago, Daxu came to prominence in the Ming Dynasty, though most of the surviving architecture dates back to the late Qing period.

Said to be one of the four famous ancient towns in Guangxi, it was Daxu's strategic location on the Li River that made it a natural trading hub. Indeed, the remnants of **13 old docks** can still be discerned along the riverbank, while the ancient town's main flagstone thoroughfare follows the contours of the waterway for two and a half kilometres, testament to the importance of this ancient highway.

This is a great place to simply amble about and take in the scene of a China that is distinctly closer to its past than its future. Many of the wooden slate roofed houses are still inhabited by old folk, while

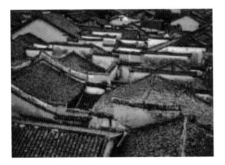

a few enterprising locals have converted their homes into handicraft stalls, hotels or cafes.

Behind the architecture highlights include, the **Hanhuang**, **Gaozu** and **Longevity** temples. The timeworn single arched **Longevity Bridge** built during the Ming Dynasty is a must see. **Maozhou Island**, located just opposite and accessible by ferry, offers a splendid space to hike through bucolic farmland. Located between the **Taiping Gate** and **Yangan Gate**, Daxu Oldest House has been meticulously preserved by the Liao family and offers a rich insight into the traditions of the past. Just opposite, **My Family Hotel** is one of the few places where you can stay in Daxu, or get a cup of coffee. The recently established **Folk Exhibition Hall** is of interest to those wishing to learn more about the ethnic minority textiles prevalent in Guilin. Strawberry picking is popular in Daxu in the springtime.

Daxu Town, Lingchuan County, Guilin (桂林市灵川县大圩镇). *Tel: 0773-2880180.*

Free admission. The bus from Guilin Bus Station to Guanyan (冠岩景区) *passes by Daxu Town. The 15km journey takes about 40mins and costs RMB6. Buses depart every 20 minutes and the last service back to Guilin departs at 18.30.*

Yangdi Town (杨堤)

Clustered on the western bank of the Li River between Guilin (about 45km) and Yangshuo, the 3,000 resident village of Yangdi is at the heart of karst country. Yangdi is most frequently visited as a starting point for boat trips along the Li River. The town's beautiful location is presented as the Guilin bus turns off the main Yangshuo road and weaves down towards the river between steep hills and through charming villages. The Yangdi bus stops beside a wide square of restaurants, toilets, and vendors of snacks and raincoats.

The dusty township isn't remarkable; however, the surrounding countryside has all the charms of rural life with farmers tilling their rice paddies, water buffalos in the fields and ample birdlife. Around Yangdi Town is the **Gong Drum Shoal** (锣鼓滩), **White Tiger Hill** (白虎山) and the **Yangdi Flying Waterfall** (水帘洞). The distance between Yangshuo and Yangdi Town can be cycled and surprisingly the small rafts accommodate bicycles too.

Yangdi Ferry, inside the Li River Scenic Area, Yangdi Town, Yangshuo County,Guilin (桂林阳朔杨堤乡漓江风景区内)*. Yangdi Town is on a local road off National Highway G321 or G65 from Guilin to Yangshuo, Gaotian and Baisha.*

Direct buses making the one hour (or longer!) trip from Guilin to Yangdi leave from the Central Bus Station in Guilin and cost RMB20.

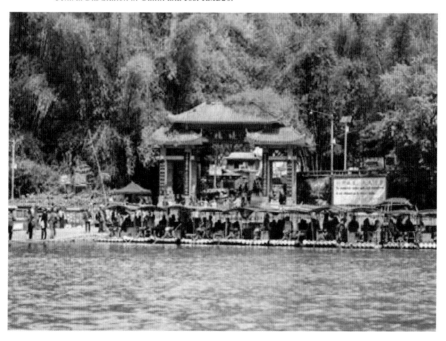

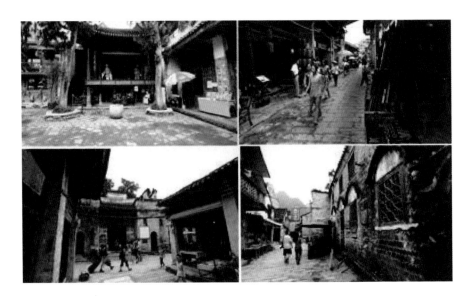

Xingping ancient town (兴坪古镇)

Hugging the Li River 27 km upstream from Yangshuo, Xingping offers many of the same virtues as China's backpacker mecca. As Yangshuo fills up with Chinese tour groups, Xingping's laid back vibe and even better scenery has increasing appeal. The countryside around Xingping now blossoms with retreats adapted from old farmhouses and kitted out for Yangshuo refuseniks.The opening of the **Yangshuo High Speed Rail Station** in the Spring of 2016 may provide a further boost, as the station is actually nearer to Xingping.

Xingping is flat and can be traversed on foot in around 15 minutes, although rental bikes are ubiquitous. Small hostels, restaurants and cafes have sprung up everywhere making Xingping perhaps reminiscent of the Yangshuo of 20 years ago. Some, like the **Master Café** on the **Old Street**, occupy interesting old buildings with wood roofs and latticed windows. The scruffy modern roads around the old centre are seeded with guest houses and travel agencies.

The town's Old Street is, unsurprisingly, where most of the town's historic buildings are found. Slap in its middle is **Wushu Temple**, which claims a history of 1800 years. The temple is now a local history museum whose exhibits include a display about the **Bai Yue** people of southern China. Admission to the museum is RMB10. Xingping also boasts a Qing vintage **Guandi Temple**, just round the corner.

Xingping's centrepiece is the broad **waterfront** with its beautiful views of the Li and **Yi** rivers.Walk right along the river for 10 minutes to come to the twenty yuan note scene (see page 70.) The **Birds' Nest Pavilion** at the southern end of the Yi waterfront also gives spectacular views but be warned that it is a 220 metre (1159 step) climb up uneven steps. The ladder section is particularly vertiginous but the small pavilion at the end is a good place to rest.

Another popular activity is to hike (or raft) along the Li River to the **Fishing Village** (渔

村). There isn't much to see there but the route passes beautiful valleys, karst landscapes and orange groves. A one-way bamboo raft costs around RMB80.

Regular buses run to Xingping from Yangshuo (until about 6pm). The 45 min journey costs a mere RMB7.50. All Yangshuo to Guilin buses pass through Xingping from where the fare is RMB20. You can also get here by bamboo boat from Yangdi or Yangshuo. Meanwhile it is also possible (just) to cycle from Yangshuo to Xingping. See pxx.

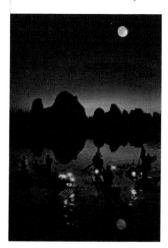

Laozhai Hill
（老寨山）

Just south of Xingping, down the river towards Yangshuo, Laozhai Hill overlooks Xingping and the horseshoe bend of the Li River. At dawn, Laozhai has a glorious aspect of the **Li River** to the east, while before dusk a magnificent view of the local rice paddy fields to the west. A photographer's dream, Laozhai Hill has a panoramic vantage for taking spectacular photos from Xingping. Laozhai Shan is about 300 meters high and takes about 20-40 minutes to ascend up the stairway to the pavilion on the summit.

Get a bus from Yangshuo to Xingping and then transfer onto a local bus from Xingping to Laozhai Shan. Free admission.

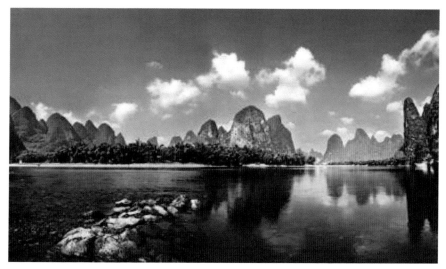

Fuli Town (福利镇)

Fuli Ancient Town, a scruffily endearing Li River village famous as the home of the Chinese painted paper fan, can be found a 15 minute drive along the **Yangshuo to Xingping road**. New Fuli, which sprawls both sides of the main road, is also rapidly being rebranded as a 'historic town'. Visitors may also arrive in the old town by bamboo raft from Xingping, Yangshuo or **Puyi**.

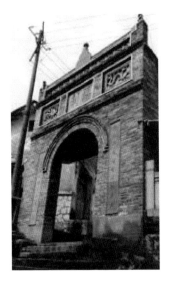

Fuli was a frequently used port of the Zhujiang river system. Despite the coaches weaving precariously through narrow lanes, Fuli's reinvention as tourist destination is a work in progress. The main street is unpretentious and the back alleys full of unrenovated but interesting old buildings. Fuli's waterfront is undeniably attractive thanks to stone balustrades and a scene of trees and mountains opposite. Motorised rafts offer excursions to Xingping and Yangshuo but the most popular service is a return trip to **Puyi Fishing Village**.

Fuli Ancient Town lies about 1.5km from the sprawl of New Fuli Town along the main road to Xingping. At the new town crossroads by the bank, turn south and head down towards the river where the old town is clustered.

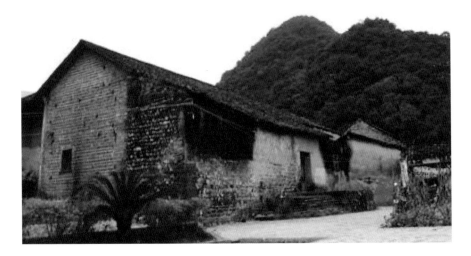

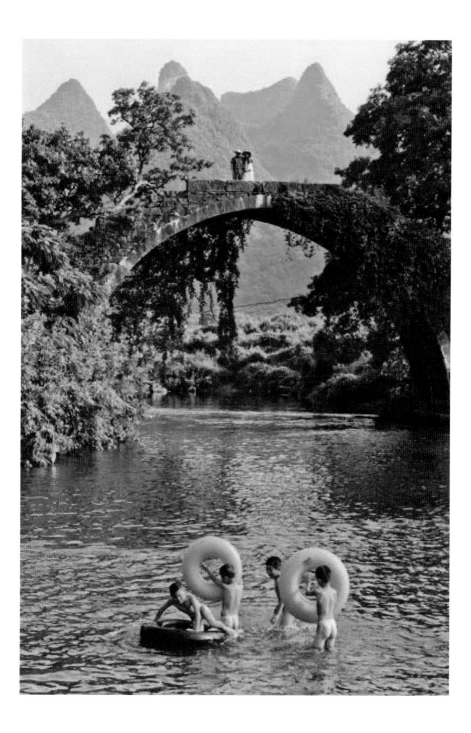

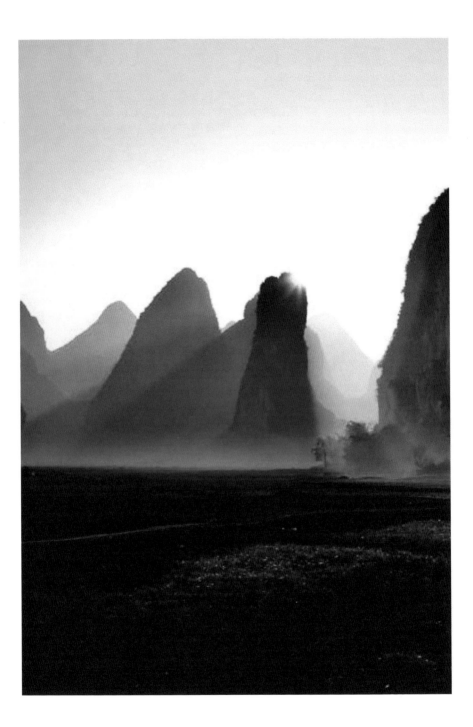

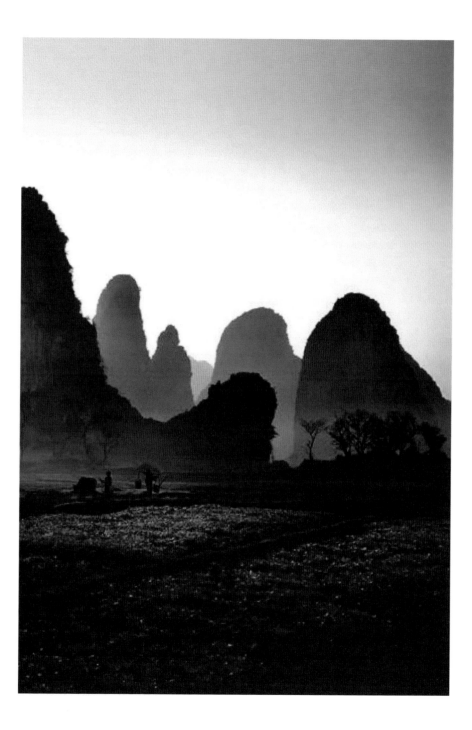

5 Yangshuo

It may be said that Guilin's scenery is 'best in the realm' according to the Chinese aphorism; however, it is also said that Yangshuo's scenery is best in Guilin. The bustle on the main thoroughfare, the pedestrian walking street of West Street, is just a testament to Yangshuo's popularity as one of China's top tourism hangouts.

IDYLLIC Yangshuo nestles snug between karst peaks on the east bank of the meandering Li River near the confluence with the Yulong River. The secret of the charming hamlet of Yangshuo has long been out, with a throng of Chinese and foreign tourists pacing the town. From top to bottom, **West Street** (西街) is lined with handicraft gift shops and laid back eateries and bars. Be sure to haggle with local vendors and don't be too surprised if local Chinese, including seniors, have some command of English. Yangshuo may be a mecca for backpackers, party-goers, sightseers, and climbers but only a short distance outside the township, Yangshuo County still possesses the allure of its natural scenery and rural life. Easily accessible is the "**Ten Li Picture Gallery**" several kilometres to the southeast, making Yangshuo an excellent base for exploring the county's peaks, caves and river ways. The road from Guilin to Yangshuo has been a bumpy ride in the past; however, the road is currently being upgraded with a number of sections completed and others still being constructed.

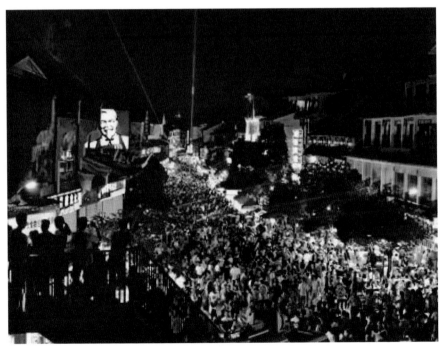

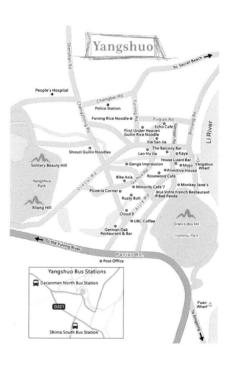

Yangshuo

To Secret Beach

Shenshan Rd.

People's Hospital

Chengbei Rd.

Police Station

Chengzhong Rd.

Furong Rice Noodle

Furong Rd.

Fugian Rd.

Echo Café

First Under Heaven
Guilin Rice Noodle

Binjiang Rd.

Li River

Xie San Jie

The Balcony Bar

Shouzi Guilin Noodles

Lao Hu Jia

Kaya

House Lizard Bar

Ganga Impression

Mojo

Yangshuo
Wharf

Solitary Beauty Hill

Primitive House

Rosewood Café

Diecui Rd.

Bike Asia

Guihua Rd.

Yangshuo
Park

Minority Cafe'7

Monkey Jane's

Pizzeria Corner

Le Votre French Restaurant

Xilang Hill

Rusty Bolt

Bad Panda

Cloud 9

UBC Coffee

Green Lotus Hill

German Oak
Restaurant & Bar

Shanshu Park

To the Yulong River

Pantao Rd.

Post Office

Yangshuo Bus Stations

Dacunmen North Bus Station

G321

Shima South Bus Station

Fuan
Wharf

To Xingping Rd.

Orientation

If you reach Yangshuo by cruise ship from Guilin, you'll disembark at the door running along **Binjiang Avenue** that runs perpendicular to West Street.

Central Yangshuo is an exciting frenetic place centred on the flagstone **West Street** (西街). Once West Street was the only tourist street in Yangshuo, but the town has now expanded with the parallel walking street **Guihua Road** and the roadways **Diecui Lu** and **Pantao Lu**. Near identical low-end hotels, souvenir stores and noisy, commercial bars dominate this main tourist drag – in peak seasons the street can become so clogged that it becomes one large queue. There are some diamonds within this rough however, including many of the town's best eateries and bars such as **Cloud Nine** and **Le Votre**.

Nonetheless for many tourists, the best thing about central Yangshuo is that you can escape it and re-visit it when you need laundry done or a gift for your mother. Ten minutes' walk in any direction from the centre takes you to the backstreets of the town, where prices fall as quality rises.

Meanwhile a swift ride on one of the many motorbike-taxis takes you to some of the most beautiful countryside in the whole county. To the north of the town, beyond the ferry pier, you can find secluded roads under bamboo fronded canopies, a charming beach, paddies galore and beautiful old hamlets. To the south is the developed tourist strip of the **Ten Li Picture Gallery** (十里画廊) – with its neon-lit caves, ethnic minority dances dressed as cavemen and a dwarf theme park. But even here there are occasional silver linings such as the **Gallery Inn**. Out to the east, we recommend the cycling trails around the new **Yulong River** eco-tourist zone, as well as rafting opportunities and a range of villages to explore. For something more authentic, head west across the Li River bridge and try out any of the options available in villages on the main road to **Xingping**.

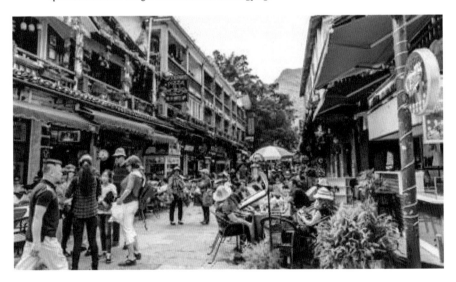

Top Eight Things To Do In Yangshuo

1. **Secret Beach.**(双滩) The top chill-out spot for locals and expats in-the-know: a clean and clear stretch of the Li River, with pristine beaches and green-land nestled against bamboo-lined banks just a kilometre north of the **ferry pier**. In summer just after midday a local farmer rents out tractor tyres for **tubing**. At RMB10 per day it's a great way to while away some time. Why not make a day of it and bring your own beer and picnic?

2. **TV Tower.** (电视塔) The highest viewpoint in town and the best place to get a sweeping view of Yangshuo and its surroundings. The walk up is punctuated by signs reading 'Do not enter', but don't fear – once you reach the summit you are allowed in on condition that you buy (much needed) a bottle of water for RMB10 from the man manning the TV station. Consider sleeping up here to take incredible dawn photos.

3. **Motorcycling.** To see far-flung sites while avoiding expensive tour-taxis and to really get a feel for the hundreds of miles of stunning karst peaks, serene paddy fields and general Arcadian-ness that this region has to offer, why not hire a **motorbike**? At RMB100 a day for a petrol-powered machine or just RMB50 for an **electric bike**, it's a steal. For those seeking greater tranquility, there are also many great **cycle paths** (see page xxx) and peddle bikes can rent for as little as RMB20 per day.

4. **Climbing.** Climbing fanatics from the world over have begun to settle here to make the most of its incredible climbing opportunities. Right now there are hundreds of **charted rock faces** and more are being made by the day, so climbing opportunities abound. A few businesses have set up to cater to this demand; for those interested in spending a day on the rockface, **Blue Sky** at No.8 Furong Road would be a good first stop.

5. **Old villages.** Yangshuo many ancient villages are often over-looked by visitors stupefied by the area's postcard perfect beauty. Those who do visit, tend to bypass some of the real gems in favour of the better-known **Xingping** and **Fuli** towns. There are actually a range of surprisingly unscathed old townships in the close vicinity of Yangshuo. Go to **Jiuxian** to see cultural revolution era graffiti daubed on the walls of 'feudal' manor houses, glimpse one of what must be China's few remaining intact ancestral worship halls (currently commemorating a Sino-Japanese war hero) and finish your trip with a visit to a beautifully restored Chinese mansion-cum-hotel (**Secret Garden**). Travel to nearby **Xiatang** for another beautifully restored manor house, the one-time family seat of a kungfu knight. Behind it find the ruins of what locals claim was variously a western-style Republican school/Japanese Brothel/PRC Commune and marvel at the stunning path connecting this village to the main road, finish your trip at the café on the main road and relax with a stunning view of an ancient bridge style and paddies. Meanwhile the aptly named **Stone City** is rumoured to have once been the imperial hide-out of an exiled dynasty, though it may well just be

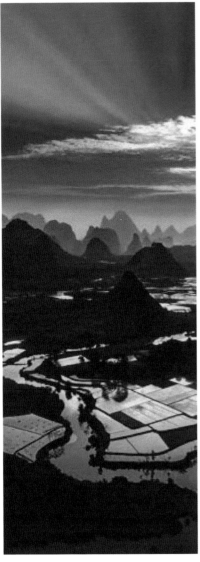

the ruins of a local minority's township. Who knows, now all that remains are charming old walls conveniently located close to the stunning **Xianggong Hill** view point.

6. **Monkey Jane's Rooftop Bar** (背包客栈). The cheapest place to spend your entire night immersed in South East Asian backpacker vibes: sip fermented snake liquor, down fresh snake blood shots and lose at **beer pong** to the hostess Jane. Thronging crowds of backpackers, good prices and Yangshuo's longest opening hours have made this into one of Yangshuo's favourite drinking-holes. Below the bar there is a sizable hostel with some of the cheapest hostel beds in town. The **rooftop bar** is deserted during the day and is a quick and easy place to get a 360 view of central Yangshuo and surrounding Karsts. Those seeking a calmer scene with better music might consider **Bad Panda** or **Mojo** next door.

7. **Boating.** "There is nothing half so much doing as messing about in boats..." (to quote from *Wind in the Willows*) and Yangshuo has ample opportunities for this. Whether you wish to go darting up and down the Li River in a faux bamboo plastic speedboat, or take a **bamboo raft** up and down the dykes of the Yulong, or perhaps go **white-water rafting** north of Xingping, options abound. Days out **tubing** on the river can be arranged at Monkey Jane's, or tubes can be hired on the Secret Beach.

8. **Stay longer.** Opportunities to lengthen a sojourn are plentiful; consult Monkey Jane for flexible bar work exchange or get in touch with **www.go-to.co** who set up volunteer-ships at any of the town's schools. For those seeking **tai chi** courses speak to the **Yangshuo Traditional Tai Chi School**, for **Chinese** lessons contact **Omeida**, and for **cooking classes** look up to **Cloud 9**.

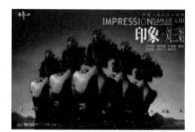

Impressions Liu Sanjie

The **Impressions Liu Sanjie** light-show is a glitzy musical performed most nights during the tourist season. Directed by acclaimed director Zhang Yimou, the show is (very) loosely based on China's top blockbuster of the Mao era, a 'The Sound of Music' style-tale following the efforts of Third Sister Liu to fight the power and foment rebellions through the medium of mountain-song (folk songs). Curiously, this is the show that puts Yangshuo on the map for Chinese tourists – it was designed to force day-trippers coming in on the boat from Guilin to spend a night in town so they could see it. The ploy certainly worked, as it is now regularly sells out, according to the local government. The show has been held directly responsible for the numbers of Chinese tourists coming through on package tours soaring from 30,000 in the 1980s to around 1.75mn today.

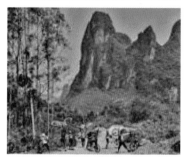

The Li River Mountain-Water Theater, Yangshuo County,Guilin (阳朔漓江山水剧场 *). Tel:0773-8811983. www.yxlsj.com*
Performances each day (weather permitting) at 19.00 and 20:30. Tickets are RMB 198/238/320/ and President's Seat RMB 480/680. Children under 1.2m have free admission but no seat. It is best to buy a ticket from a travel agency or hotel since they will usually provide a car to drive you to the theatre.

Li River Motor Boating

The Li River features 'rafts' made out of fake bamboo, powered by two-stroke outboards. These dart up and down the river to the south of Yangshuo Town and will take in a photo shoot opportunity somewhere along the way. These boats charge a premium to show you the karst hills of Yellow Cloth Shoal depicted on the RMB20 note, so we suggest avoiding this tourist trap and instead just enjoying the other worldly scenery anywhere else on the river.

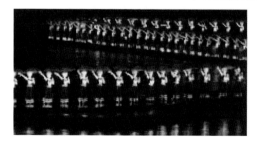

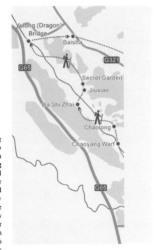

The Yulong River (遇龙河)

Overview

For many, biking, hiking or boating the Yulong River valley is the highlight of a Yangshuo visit. This Li River tributary runs for 35km from northern Yangshuo County near **Litang** through small villages including **Gaotian** and **Jiuxian**, before emptying into the Li River near **Pingle**. The Yulong's charm is enhanced because there are no motorised boats, only pole-propelled bamboo rafts. Outside the scattering of villages, there are also few businesses or services, in part because the river is prone to flooding. The river is shallow, with an average depth of 5m, and clean as it weaves through a largely agricultural area of rice fields and cash crops such as pomelos and mandarin oranges. On the river are a number of **weirs**, although some have fallen into disrepair. It is possible to boat over a few, and in winter you can walk across them.

The Yulong River scenic area is a 5km cycle ride from Yangshuo through pleasant agricultural land. Another option is to get a taxi from town and hire a bike at one of many outlets along the river. Meanwhile attractive guesthouses have sprung up here, making it a plausible alternative to staying in town.

Along the river are several cycling and hiking and boating routes which it is common to combine, for example, taking a stretch by raft, while your bike is transported to the other end. Some of the best cycling and hiking is around the **Gaotian Village** area, which includes the **Moon Hill** hike and **Butterfly Cave**. Here there are also guesthouses, and several ancient villages to explore.

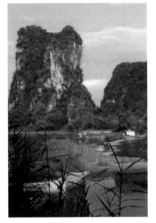

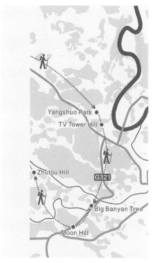

Three ferry docks and two major bridges, **Jiuxian Bridge** and **Yulong Bridge**, make common staging points for the Yulong River bike or hike itineraries. Boats are piloted and it is not permitted to charter them independently. Because of the system of weirs, at some ferries return routes are offered, while elsewhere it is only possible to travel one way and pick up your bike at the other end. It is not allowed to take bikes on boats.

Boating

It's popular to rent real chauffeured bamboo raft-punts on the Yulong River. These either take you on a lap of a section of the Yulong or for the more intrepid, they can take you across one of the dykes for a splash. In peak seasons, these trips are more about photo opportunities than having a relaxing cruise. Night-time boat trips can also be arranged for those hoping to glimpse cormorant fishing or enjoy black-market viewings of **Liu Sanjie** lightshow.

The four main Yulong bamboo boat routes are:

1 Xiatang Wharf（金宝码头）to Jinbao Wharf （金宝桥）. Xiatang is the most popular ferry with tour groups. Boats embarking from Xiatang offer a return trip to Jinbao Wharf. The river is at its most crowded here, with bamboo rafts lined end-to- end like on a conveyer belt.

2. Chaoyang Wharf（朝阳码头）to Gongnong Bridge（工农桥）. The route beween Chaoyang Wharf and Gongnong Bridge arguably offers the best river views.

3. Shui e di（水厄底码头）to Gongnong Bridge. One way.

4. Yulong Bridge to Jiuxian. One way.

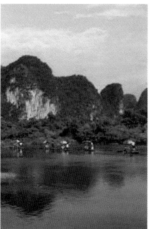

Cycling

With flat winding country paths snaking through scenery comprising of majestic peaks, winding rivers and ancient villages, it's as if the bicycle was invented to explore Guilin. Cycling is by far the best way to enjoy the majesty of the region, especially Yangshuo and the Li and Yulong river valleys.

Bicycle hire is near ubiquitous in Yangshuo. Most guesthouses offer bike rental service of some description. At the low end expect to pay around RMB20 for a rusty roadster, whereas RMB120 at the other end of the scale will get you a serious mountain bike. Unless you're simply pottering down to **Moon Hill** and back, make sure your two-wheeler has gears, thick tyres and suspension, as the best fun is to be off-the-beaten-path.

Australian-run **Bike Asia** is a well-recommended, all-inclusive bike rental shop with many years' experience working in the area. Centrally located on **Guihua Street**, a host of quality bikes suitable for all expectations are available to hire. **Bike Asia** can also arrange guided bike tours, with everything from serious of- road adventure to family friendly rides.

For more info go to: www.bikeasia.com or email: info@bikeasia. Tel: 0773-8826521.

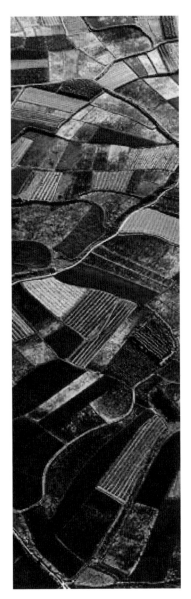

Bike Routes

First make sure you have all the safety provision including a quality bike, helmet, puncture repair kit, a map, suitable clothing for the weather, and emergency phone numbers. Then rent a bike. It's that simple. The best way to explore Yangshuo is to just hop on your bike and go. The more you get lost, the more wonders you'll stumble upon. That said it makes sense to follow a specified route if you haven't got too much time to waste, if you are travelling alone and want to stay safe or with a group with expectations to see the top sites. Below are three of the top tried-and-tested bicycle routes to consider.

1. The Yulong River Circuit (遇龙河环行)

Time needed: Half day.
Distance: 15km.
Option: Put your bike on a bamboo raft at **Chaoyang Warf** and ride the water.

This is the probably the Yangshuo ride you've been dreaming about. It's not too tough, but still opt for a mountain bike if possible, as some roads are nothing more than gravel tracks. Follow the road south past the sister villages of **Chaoyang** (朝阳) and **Chaolong** (朝隆). Nearby you'll find the river and bamboo rafters here but veer away from the water towards **Jiuxian** (旧县), the prettiest and best preserved ancient village on the river. If you're planning to stop for a coffee break, Jiuxian has a few cafes to choose from as well as the foreign run **Secret Garden** (秘密花园) boutique hotel. From here on keep to the tracks and head towards **Baisha** (白沙), a local market town. Nearby is Yulong, a gorgeous riverside locale famed for the Yulong (Dragon) Bridge, which dates back to the Ming Dynasty. Here you can cross the water and make your return to Yangshuo on the other side of the river. Keep pedalling until you get to **Da Shi Zhai** (大石寨) from where it's best to cross back to Jiuxian on one of two bridges. Alternatively keep going past Chaoyang Dock towards **Zhutou Hill**(猪头山) and make **Moon Hill** (月亮山) and the **Big Banyan Tree** (大榕树风景区) part of your circuit.

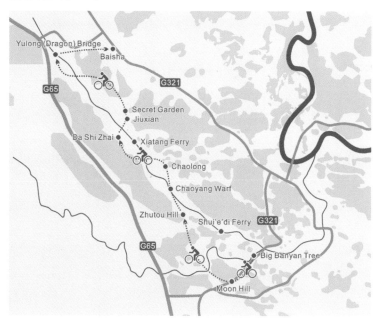

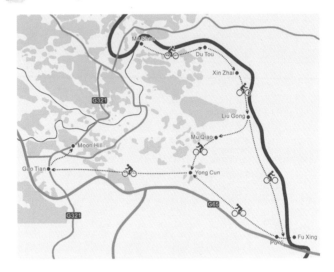

5 Yangshuo

2. Yangshuo Villages Circuit (阳朔县线路)

Time needed: Half a day.
Distance: 26km
Options: Stop for lunch and hire a canoe in Liu Gong.

This is a lovely ride as it takes you away from the main roads for the most part. Follow the Li River east out of Yangshuo to the village of **Mu Shan** (木山). Then you simply village-hop from **Du Tou** (渡头), **Xin Zhai** (新寨) stopping to photograph the pastoral scenery as you go. At the riverside village of **Liu Gong** (留公) you'll find canoe hire, boats back to Yangshuo, some peasant family eateries and an ancient tower. It's a great place to stop for lunch and look out across the river. Nearby you should also check out the three-colour ponds. Then continue through **Mu Qiao** (木桥). You'll have to hit the main road for a stretch but at **Yong Cun** (勇村) it's back to country paths. When you reach **Moon Hill** (月亮山) veer north back into town.

This circuit won't take a day. If you're interested in staying in the saddle for a full eight hours, at Yong Cun you can make an excursion and add the twin ancient towns of **Pu Yi** (普益) and **Fu Xing** (福兴) part of your tour. **Gao Tian** (高田), south of Moon Hill, is also a possible additional destination. Alternatively, if you maintain a good pace, why not merge the village circuit with Yulong River circuit?

3. Yangshuo to Xingping (阳朔 - 兴坪)

Time needed: A day.
Distance: 26km (one way).
Options: Come back on the regular buses between Xingping and Yangshuo.

Though it's 25km to Xingping by road, following the trails it can feel more like 50km. A fit and experienced mountain biker could get there and back in a day but for the rest of us, consider staying over in **Xingping** (or Yangshuo if you're departing from Xingping). It's also recommended to take a guide with you, as this ride requires a boat river crossing and a lot of dirt mountain paths. That said, it's an awesome ride, and will doubtlessly be the Yangshuo experience that resonates with you long after you've departed.

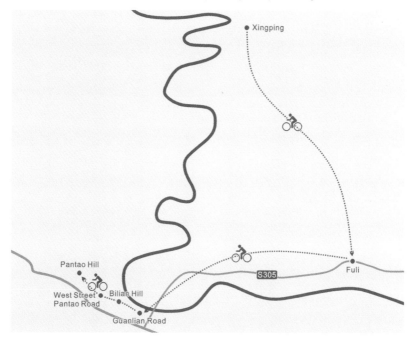

If you go without a guide you best follow the roads and travel via **Fuli** (福 利). From West Street turn left on **Pantao Road** (蟠桃路) and continue for 400 meters until you pass between **Pantao Hill** (蟠桃山) and **Bilian** (碧莲山). Here turn left onto **Guanlian Road** (观莲路). After 600 meters keep right and you will come to some concrete vehicle barriers with gaps for bicycles. Here you can join Provincial Road S305 (省道 305). Turn left on the S305 and follow it across the Li River. After just over 6km a steep right bend marks the edge of the market town Fuli. It's worth spending some time in Fuli (see page 77). The road from Fuli to Xingping is the X094, a narrow two-way road with quite a lot of tourist bus traffic.

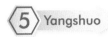

Hiking

With thousands of limestone peaks in Guilin, there are abundant hikes up the karst hills, as well as countryside trails that take in rural life of Guilin. There are many established parks with pagodas or pavilions adorning the peak, as well as some untouched summits to scale.

It is possible to engage a **local guide** to help navigate the fields and peaks of Guilin and price is negotiable. All trails are not necessarily clearly marked and the assistance of a local guide can assist in finding the right path. It should be noted, that it is not always clear whose property hikes traverse and local farmers' fields should be respected.

In places, the locals have an uncanny knack of being en route with food and drink, umbrellas and rain jackets in the wet. Sometimes they can pester hikers by following them along the hike and insisting on a fee – they should be politely ignored.

When scaling peaks in Guilin, care should be taken due to some trails varying in the degree of maintenance. Steps can be slippery or loose tiles and rocks can fall from the steep mountains.

Scenic Spots Around Yangshuo

Moon Hill (月亮山)

Moon Hill, also known as **"Bright Moon Peak"**, is a must see limestone formation in Yangshou's Ten Li Picture Gallery. The 50m high natural archway, which has been likened to the moon, is on top of the 380-meter hill. It takes between 20-40 minutes to reach the summit where you can enjoy views of the **Jinbao River valley**. Meanwhile the opposite side of the road is a popular site for photographs with Moon Hill in the background.

The end of Ten Li Picture Gallery, Fenglou Village, Gaotian Town, the western side of Guilin high-speed road, Yangshuo (阳桂荔公路西侧高田乡凤楼村，朔十里画廊末端 *). Opening hours from 7:00-18:30. Entrance is RMB15 & RMB5 to climb the mountain.*

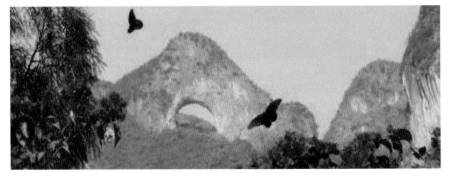

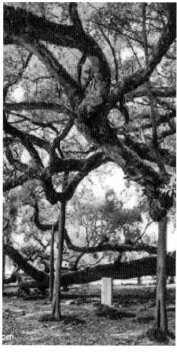

Yangshuo Park (阳朔公园)

In the centre of Yangshuo Town is Yangshuo Park. This conveniently located park is a popular spot for locals practicing tai chi, playing mah-jong or dancing in the morning and evening. The park has a small lagoon and a winding stairway to the summit of **Man Hill (Xilang)**. With a pavilion on top it has a bird's eye view of Yangshuo. Man Hill is said to be a guy bowing to the nearby **Lady Hill (Xiaogu)**.

Also close to downtown Yangshuo is **Dragon Head Hill (龙头山)**, which can be seen from the cruise ships as they enter Yangshuo.

Diecui Rd, Yangshuo (阳朔叠翠路).
Open from 09:00-17:00. Free admission.

The Big Banyan Tree (大榕树风景区)

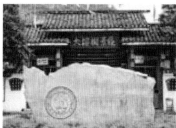

The more than one thousand year old 'Big Banyan Tree' grows on the western banks of the **Jinbao River** about seven kilometres outside of Yangshuo in **Gaotian Town** in the **Big Banyan Tree Park**. Reputedly planted in the Sui dynasty, the gigantic canopy tree covers 1,000 square meters, is 17 meters high, and has a girth of seven meters.

Sunlight doesn't penetrate the shady tree's glossy leaves. The tree has a twisted and gnarly truck with a long branch protruding only one meter above the ground propped up by aerial roots.

The Big Banyan Tree was immortalized in the 1960s film *Liu Sanjie*, in which lovers declare their feelings under the tree's umbrella. As a result, the tree is a magnet for young couples and film buffs.

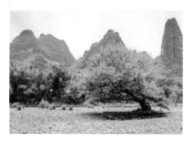

Guiyang Road, G321 National Road, Gaotian Town, Yangshuo (阳朔高田镇 G321 国道桂阳公路). The park is open from 07.00 – 18.30. Admission is RMB20. Take the bus from Yangshuo to Gaotian Town or bike it.

94

Popular Walks and Hikes

TV Tower Hill（电视台山）

Take a short stroll down **Pantao Road** to the **China Postal Saving Bank**, then turn into the alleyways that zigzag towards TV Tower Hill with its commanding views of Yangshuo. Hiking TV Tower Hill involves about a 45-minute scramble up the steep mountain to the town's local broadcast tower. Don't be put off by the "No entry" sign at the top, as for RMB5 the security guard will let you in for a 360-degree view.

Off Pantao Rd, Yangshuo（阳朔蟠桃路）*near the second pedestrian overpass away from West Street.*

Along the Yulong River to the Dragon Bridge

Following a similar trail as a popular **Yulong River** cycling route, the countryside walk along the river takes in the agricultural life of Yangshuo at a slower pace. Pass through historic **Jiuxian Village** towards the 400 year old **Yulong Bridge** for a swim in the river. The walk takes at least three hours but rafts down the Yulong are an option for the return trip.

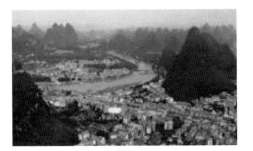

Climbing

With its thousands of **karst peaks**, Guilin is a mecca for rock climbers who come from around the world to scale the crags and cliff faces. The first local peaks were mastered by German climbers in the mid-1980s. Then routes were opened up by American and Chinese climbers in the early 1990s. Now there are over 800 sports climbing routes.

Guilin's popularity is based upon the **many and varied routes**, the quality of the rock, the accessibility of the peaks and its low cost. 'Sports' or 'single pitch' climbing involves utilising permanently anchored points already bolted into the cliff face. '**Traditional**' or 'free' rocking climbing requires climbers to temporarily fix anchor points (known as cams) as they 'multi-pitch' climb.

From the experienced team of Tyson Wallace and Paul Qui, the Guilin climbers' bible is the book **Yangshou Rock Climbers**, first published in 2003 and now in its twelfth edition. The book features extensive maps of locations, climbing routes on each rock wall, difficulty ratings, and advice about sun and rain exposure. A copy of the book can be purchased (RMB120) or used for reference at any of the rock climbing clubs or inns in Yangshuo.

The majority of the climbs in and around Yangshuo are sports climbs, where the lead climber must free or solo climb to the next bolt to anchor the rope. There are also a number of 'top rope' climbs, where a rope is anchored first from the top of the cliff and provides an extra degree of safety for beginners.

Many of the rock climbing mountains are only accessed by crossing fields and

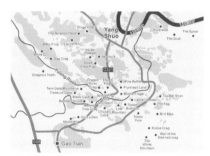

climbers should take not to disturb local farmers and should stick to existing pathways. Though rock climbing in Yangshuo is considered to be 'free'', it has been known for locals to attempt to charge climbers for access across farmland.

The peak season for rock climbing in Yangshuo is in the **dryer months** from October until early December, as mid-summer can be hot, winter cold and spring wet.

Getting Ready

Rock climbing can be a hazardous sport, and it is essential to have professional equipment and guides for novices, or at the very least an experienced **belayer** in the group. All of the Yangshuo rock climbing clubs provide professional rock climbing guides and equipment hire for those new to the sport.

Prices for **equipment** vary from club to club with other variables including time, distance to the climbing location and amount of kit hired (approximately RMB300 / half day). Rock climbing gear can also be purchased from climbers' inns and the pro shop **Kailas** (in Yangshuo and Guilin); however, the store sadly doesn't sell rock climbing shoes.

Many experienced rock climbers bring their own **equipment** to Yangshuo, including dynamic rope, quick draws, belay devices, a harness, chalk bag, helmet and **climbing shoes**. Experienced climbers new to Yangshuo usually make new friends at one of the **rock climbing inns** and go in groups to rock faces.

The tight-knit Yangshuo rock climbing community pioneers new routes, and ensures the safety and maintenance of routes as well as the cleanliness of the general cliff area. Yangshuo's **Rockabond Climbing Bar** also has a bouldering wall, and artificial indoor climbing wall, so you could warm up before attempting an outdoor climb.

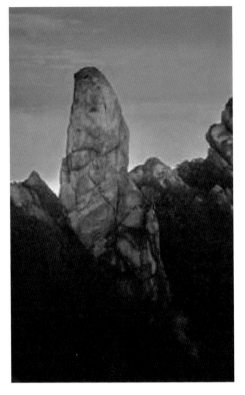

Yangshuo Crags

Swiss Cheese (瑞士奶酪)

Close to Yangshuo Town, down a village lane before the northern gate to the **Ten Li Picture Gallery**, is the aptly named **Swiss Cheese** crag. The pockmarked karst cliff is excellent for lower to intermediate climbers with its thirteen different routes varying from 10 to 35 meters in height, plus another eight routes on another face.

Swiss Cheese is a short walk through fields and past a local hotel with refreshments. The base of the cliff is shaded by a grove of bamboo. Also in the general vicinity is the euphemistically named, phallic looking peak called Jeremy's Jiji which is the fastest top out in Yangshuo. With three routes, Jeremy's Jiji has commanding views of the valley. Meanwhile on the other side of the field are the **Three Little Pigs** (三只小猪) with nine more routes and a more challenging crag with an overhang.

Wine Bottle (酒瓶山), Middle Finger (中指峰) and Thumb Peak (拇指峰)

Several hundred meters across a field opposite **Butterfly Park Cave** is the **Wine Bottle** cliff named for a suggestively shaped peak. One of the best climbing crags in Yangshuo, Wine Bottle is easily accessible, with a multitude of climbs on quality rock; however, as it faces south it can be hot in the midday sun. With 29 routes with varying degrees of difficulties, Wine Bottle is a technical climb with a slight incline of the rock face.

About 400 meters down the road from Butterfly Park Cave is **Thumb Peak**, whose 13 routes offer some of the best multi-pitch climbing in Yangshou. The east facing Thumb Peak has routes protected from the rain and is generally shady at midday; it also has a few bolted routes.

The **Middle Finger**, on the opposite side of the road to Thumb Peak, was one of the earliest crags to be popular with climbers in Yangshuo. The challenging peak is generally the preserve of traditional climbers though newer bolted and top rope routes have been opened. With north and south facing cliffs, Middle Finger has twenty routes.

The **Promised Land** is a two-route peak located a couple hundred meters down the road from **Butterfly Park Cave**. It has a 20-meter abseiling top rope anchor point. Further down the Yangshuo to Gaotian road, near the Yulong River, are **Screaming Turtle Mountain** and **Dragon River Crag**, which each have several routes.

Riverside (师龙山)

About four kilometres on the road east out of Yangshuo, on the south bank of the Li River, is the **Riverside Crag**. Riverside has an overhanging buttress, north facing, which makes it shady and generally protected from the rain. The crag has quality rock, a top rope and 24 routes with short climbs for beginners and routes for traditional climbing. One hundred meters down the road is a crag called the Solar System with an additional four routes.

Close by to Riverside off the esplanade is **The Goat** (老杨山), with 13 routes, while several kilometres further down the river road is **The Spear** (飞镖山), a quiet and leafy seven route crag.

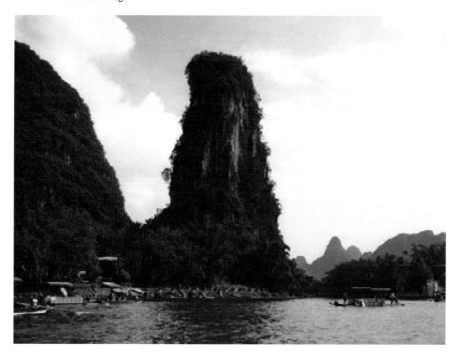

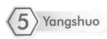

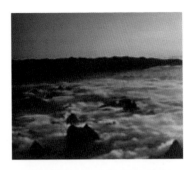

White Mountain (白山)
and The Egg (鸡蛋山)

Off the main road to **Puyi** from Yangshuo on country roads are **White Mountain** and **The Egg**, reached about two kilometres after crossing the Yulong River. You will find The Egg first, spurring off the road to Puyi before the turn to White Mountain.

With good belaying areas, the dome shaped Egg, has eastern, northern and western crags - allowing climbers to avoid the sun and rain. The Egg offers 40 different routes of varying difficulties and heights. Close to the Egg are the challenging multi-pitch climb **Tuo Bei Shan** (驼背山) and the orange cliff face **Bird Man** (鸟人山) twelve route climb.

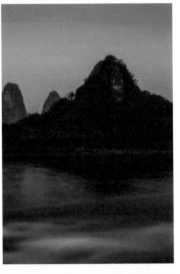

A massive 200 meter long cliff face, White Mountain is probably the most impressive crag in Yangshuo and one of the most popular for climbing. The steep overhang is up to 15 degrees off-vertical.. An all-weather crag, White Mountain has athletic climbs requiring stamina with heights of up to 60 meters, as well as technical climbs in pockets and over edges.

Also in the general area of White Mountain are the sunny **Wall of the Damned** crag and the small five-route buttress **Kiddie Crag**.

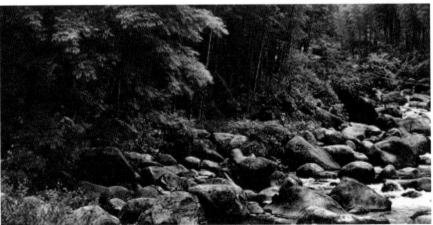

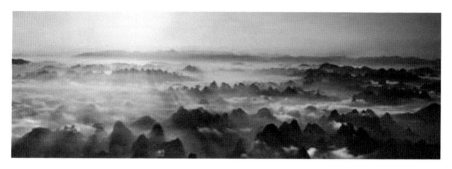

The Twin Gate Area

Off the road from Yangshuo to Gaotian Town past the **Big Banyan** Tree and in between the **Jinbao** and **Yulongr rivers** is the **Twin Gate area**. After crossing the Jinbao River from the main road and passing through a small village, the area behind the local school opens into a farming valley. The fields are hemmed in by the east by the **Treasure Cave** (穿岩藏球) and to the north by the **Twin Gate Mountains** (同门门山).

The southern face of the **Twin Gate Mountain** has two caves, which can be sunny in the morning. The caves provide shelter from the sun and rain; and offer concrete tables and chairs to relax as well as easy access to the river for swimming. The Twin Gate Mountains have quality rock and are popular with climbers, with 21 routes to scale the peak on multiple sides.

The **Treasure Cave** requires a short but sharp zigzagging ascent up the mountain to reach the two tunnel caves which pierce the peak. Inside the high caves are remains of the footings of a fortified gate and huts that were used to hide from the Japanese. The Treasure Cave is good for sheltered wet weather climbing; however, it can be quite damp and windy. The routes inside the Treasure Cave are generally top rope climbs on both sides of the cave, and it is also set up for zip lining.

Close to the road, around the back of the Big Banyan Tree Park, is the three-sided buttress, **Banyan Tree Crag**. The Banyan Tree crag has 18 routes, while close by is the four top rope crag, Bamboo Grove. Also near Banyan Tree Park is the small **Black Cave** (黑洞) - good in wet weather but with poor quality rock.

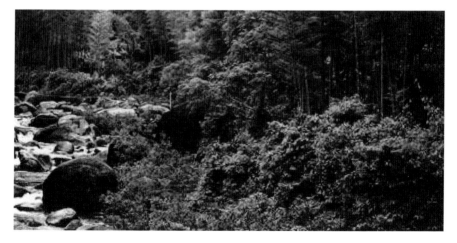

Baby Frog Area (蝌蚪山)

The Baby Frog Area is reached by following **Longyue Road** (龙岳路), aka Country Road 66, out of Yangshuo towards **Chaoyangzhai** (朝阳寨), then heading north towards **Xiatangzhai** (夏堂寨), on Country Road 90. On the northern bank of the Yulong River, near the Xiatangzhai Quay (夏堂寨码头), are the crags Baby Frog and **While Cliff** (白岩).

Baby Frog is a popular crag for lower to intermediate climbers, with its lower grades, top ropes and 17 routes. On the other side of the village from Baby Frog is the three-sided buttress, White Cliff, with 20 routes that allow for all day climbing.

Just before Xiatangzhai is the three route **Dag Crag** with two prominent overhangs, while the short, top rope route the **Dragon's Tooth** (龙牙) is accessed by crossing the river. Closer to Yangshuo along are Longyue Road crags **Dingo's Dell**, the **Neighborhood** (邻居) and **Laotie Hill**.

The short sports climb, Laotie Hill, was popular when climbing first opened in Yangshou but has since been neglected, while Dingo Dell's is a three route short climb.

Space Buttress (太空站) & Low Mountain (矮山)

After crossing the Yulong River on the **Ten Li Picture Gallery** and taking the local road east along the southern bank of the Yulong for about three kilometres you come to **Space Buttress**. This large peak has a significant overhang and is shady in the morning with 21 varied crags. The not

so short, multi-pitch **Low Mountain** is partially sheltered from even heavy rain. It can be tough in the sun however and has some loose rocks.

Behind Space Buttress is the shabby **Camel's Head** (骆头山) with its steep upper face. South of Space Buttress, the slender, two sided **Totem Pole** (图腾柱) is sunny and has seven crags. Also, on the way to Space Buttress is **Chicken Cave** (鸡窝度), one of the best crags to climb in the wet with a large protected and dry belay area.

Moon Hill (月亮山)

Climbing the icon arches of Moon Hill with its challenging overhang is a Yangshuo rock climber's dream. However, though the span has been bolted with 27 crags, climbing has been temporarily halted due to liability issues. Many a climber has still stowed their climbing gear in their backpack and climbed the iconic archway; however, climbers should really respect the local authorities and refrain from climbing.

Halfway up the trek up Moon Hill, the path diverges to **Odin's Den** (奥丁窝), a large cave with 10 crags inside and outside the cave.

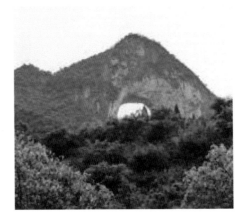

Caving

Guilin's karst topography not only extends to the spectacular pinnacles above ground, but also under the surface of the earth. Below ground Guilin also has a vast array of sinkholes, dolines (a depression, where the surface crust has collapsed), underground streams and rivers; as well as caves (the most in Guangxi).

If rainwater descends directly into the subterranean environment, calcium carbonate can form in solution to drip into caves and form stalactites hanging from the roofs of caves and stalagmites building from the floor of caves. Karst caves also form twisted rock formation called helicities which warp in all directions, pillars or columns when a stalactite and stalagmites join; and flowstones with the build-up of calcite growth.

The weathering under karst topography can also come in a variety of forms including bellholes (small domes on the ceiling), breakdowns (rubble from falling debris), flutes (elongated vertical rock on the walls), spongework (Swiss cheese shaped holes), pendants (wedged or blade shaped rocks), dripstones (speleothems); pockets; tubes; channel in-cuts and vadose canyons.

Spelunk Guides

The low-hanging fruit for spelunceans (cave explorers) in Guilin are the popular "**show caves**" generally run by State owned enterprises. Each of these well-lit caverns has paved paths, gantries, guardrails, guides and facilities.

The '**fairyland**' show caves are illuminated by multi-coloured light shows that highlight cave features. The wondrous rock shapes, pillars, curtains and waterfalls have been labelled in the idiosyncratic Chinese style as reminiscent of various fruits, gods and goddesses and aspects of nature.

However, karst caves in a tropical area like Guilin are susceptible to moisture and inside the cave is often quite wet and it can be slippery under foot. **Non-slip footwear** is essential, and a plastic bag to protect passports, phones and cameras is highly recommended especially for any caves with mud pools (plus a swimsuit and towel if you intend on taking a mud bath).

Guilin has an abundance of caves riddling the limestone mountains and the more thrill-seeking spelunkeans pursuing an adventure sports experience should seek the assistance of one of the **rock climbing clubs**. Theses caves are unregulated and you need to take responsibility for your own safety and avail yourself of an experienced guide. The most popular of these caves are the **Buddha Cave** and the **Longmen Water Cave**.

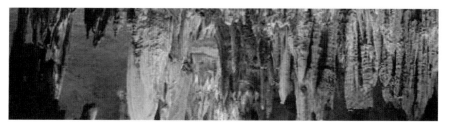

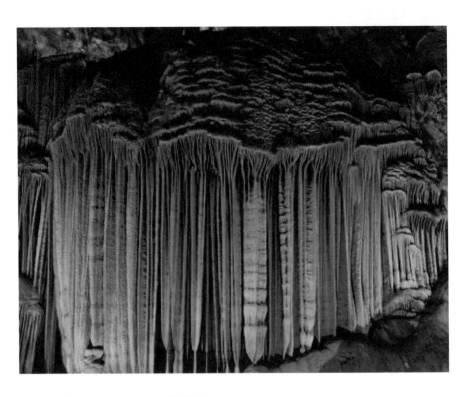

Silver Water Cave (银子岩)

In **Lipu County**, 18 kilometres from Yangshuo (85 kilometres from Guilin), the **Silver Water Cave** consists of tiers from different geological eras. The Silver Cave has an upper chamber, grand hall, and a lower chamber with supporting pillars, and an underground stream.

The Silver Cave is similar to the **Seven Star Cave** but with more extensive tunnelling under an astounding twelve mountain peaks covering a distance of two kilometres. The stalactites and stalagmites are dissolved from a mineral crystal that appears silver - giving rise to the cave's name.

The 'three sights' of Silver Cave are the **"Roaring Waterfall"** from Snow Capped Mountain, the **"Musical Stalactite Folding Screen"** and the **"Magic Reflections in the Jade Pool"**. While the cave's 'three treasurers' are the **"Preaching Buddha"**, **"Pearl Umbrella"** and **"The Towering Pillar"**.

Ligui Lu, Maling Town, Lipu County, Guilin （桂林市荔浦县马岭镇荔桂公路）. *Tel: 0773-7133582.*

Opening Hours are 08:30-17:30 and admission is RMB84. Buses to Maling Town leave from Guilin and Yangshuo.

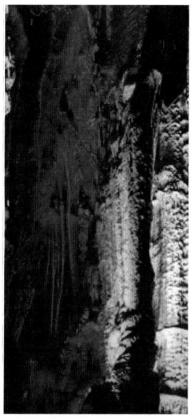

Gold Water Cave (金水岩)

Opposite Moon Hill on the Ten Li Picture Gallery, the Gold Water Cave (formerly called the **Water Cave**) is similar to other caves with incredible stalactites, stalagmites, rock formations, ponds, springs and streams. However, unique here is the **hot mud baths**. Visitors come here to frolic in the **40 degree** muddy pool - so bring a swimsuit, a towel and a plastic bag for the inevitable mud fight.

Yiling Village, Gaotain Town, Yangshuo County, Guilin (桂林市阳朔县高田镇历村金水岩景区(十里画廊内). *Tel: 07738776999. www.watercave.net*
Opening Hours are 08:00-16:00 and entrance is RMB90.

Butterfly Cave
(天籁 • 蝴蝶泉景区)

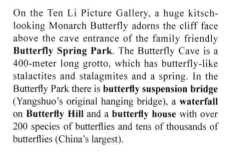

On the Ten Li Picture Gallery, a huge kitsch-looking Monarch Butterfly adorns the cliff face above the cave entrance of the family friendly **Butterfly Spring Park**. The Butterfly Cave is a 400-meter long grotto, which has butterfly-like stalactites and stalagmites and a spring. In the Butterfly Park there is **butterfly suspension bridge** (Yangshuo's original hanging bridge), a **waterfall** on **Butterfly Hill** and a **butterfly house** with over 200 species of butterflies and tens of thousands of butterflies (China's largest).

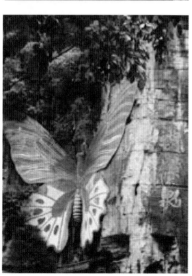

Shili Hualang, Yueliangshan Scenic Area, Gaotian Town, Yangshuo County (桂林阳朔高田镇月亮山风景区十里画廊内). *Tel: 0773-8811466.*
Opening hours are 07.00 – 18.30 and tickets are RMB60. Buses from Yangshuo to Gaotian Town stop at the Butterfly Spring Cave.

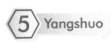

5 Yangshuo

Assembling Dragon Cave
(聚龙潭)

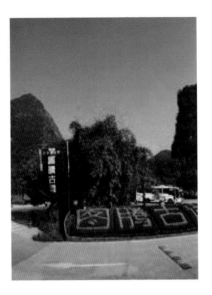

At the foot of **Horse Hill**, also along the Ten Li Picture Gallery, the Assembling Dragon Cave gets its name from the encircling mountain peaks appearing to be a dragon amongst the clouds. The **"dragon's lair"** cave is about 1000 meters long, 30 meters wide and 25 meters high and can be explored on foot or by raft on the underground stream.

The cave is popular with Chinese tourists and the antiphonal Zhuang folk song **Liu Sanjie** echoes through the cave. The Assembling Dragon Cave contains the apparently bottomless **Wudi Pool**.

Shili Hualang, Yueliangshan Scenic Area, Gaotian Town, Yangshuo County (桂林阳朔高田镇月亮山风景区十里画廊内).

Opening hours are 08.30 – 17.30 and entrance is RMB68. Buses from Yangshuo to Gaotian Town stop along the Ten Li Picture Gallery.

Buddha Cave (佛岩)

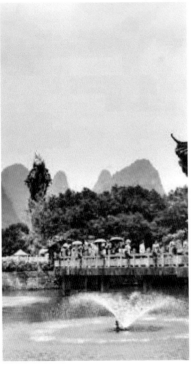

On the west bank of the Yulong River near **Baisha Town**, the three chambers of the maze-like cave **Buddha Cave** traverse three mountains. Spelunking in the Buddha cave requires squeezing between narrow rock passages, crawling through muddy holes, and climbing on ropes and ladders.

First take a boat deeper into the cave to a dry limestone area with rock formations said to look like a statue of **Maitreya Buddha**, a large mud bath and a hot spring to rinse off the mud. A shallow gravel stream with a placid flow washes through.

The Buddha Cave is on private farmland and unlike many local show caves it isn't controlled

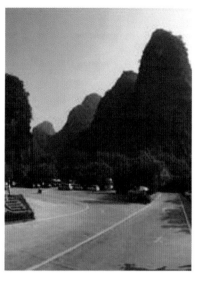

GUILIN: THE GUIDE

by a State owned enterprise. Refugees took sanctuary in the Buddha Cave during times of Japanese incursion. The cave has many branches and shouldn't be explored alone; moreover, some sections are off limits. A helmet, flashlight and batteries, and shoes with good grip are highly recommended.

Foyan Village, Baisha Town, Yangshuo (阳朔 白沙镇佛岩村).
Buses are available from Yangshuo to Baishao Town.

Lotus Cave (莲花岩)

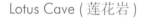

Three kilometres outside of **Xingping** is the small Lotus Cave, less than 500m long, with a bottleneck shaped entrance opening to a large chamber. The Lotus Cave has a remarkable cluster of stalactites that appear to be lotus blossoms, called the "**Lotus Petals Suspended Upside Down**". There is also a stalactite called the "**Stone Heptachord**" which when struck gives off a note.

Country Road 60, Baishadi Village, Xingping, Guilin (桂林兴坪白沙氏乡道60).
Opening hours are 09.00 – 17.00 and tickets are RMB50. Buses are available from Yangshou to Xingping.

Moon Water Cave (月亮水岩)

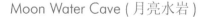

At the southern end of the Ten Li Picture Gallery, is the **Moon Water Cave**, a dimly lit rustic mud cave without karst formations. The main draw here is a mud pool which visitors wade through knee high water, climb over ledges, and duck under low ceilings to frolic in.

The mud pool is less than waist deep. Afterwards people rinse off in the hot springs. A

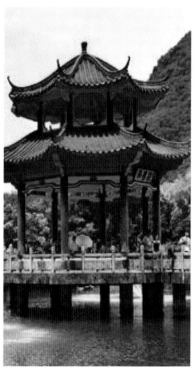

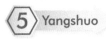

short boat ride out takes you back to the entrance where there is a watercourse to swim in.

Pingtang Village, Gaotian Town, Yangshuo (阳朔高田镇平塘村). *Entrance to the cave is RMB 90. Buses are available from Yangshuo to Gaotian Town.*
Open from 08:00-17:30.

Longmen Water Cave (龙门水岩)

On the road from **Gaotian Town** towards **Longmen Village** is the recently developed Longmen Water Cave. The cave is reached by boat across a large pond and through the lips of the cave.

The cave opens into a high cavernous hall and its four tiers burrow for three kilometres under three mountains. The Longmen Water Cave is not illuminated, requiring a torch. Passageways can be cramped and steep due to the limestone formations. There is also a mud pool and a waterfall. The cave was used as a hideout to escape the Japanese.

About 10km away from Yangshuo, located in Longmen Town, Yangshuo (阳朔龙门镇距离阳朔东南部 10km). *Entrance to the cave is RMB168*

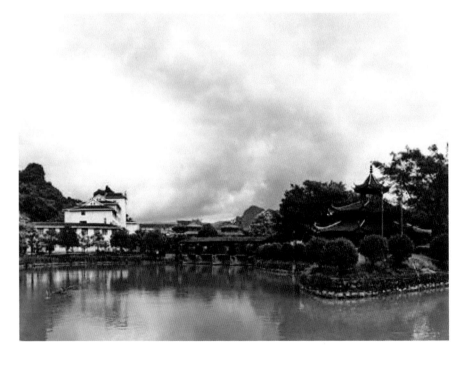

Fengyu Cave (丰鱼岩)

About 18 kilometers south of Yangshuo in **Lipu County** is the subterranean river cave Fengyu or **Blind Fish** cave. The stream teems with small fish known as 'Yaofeng and though the river' dimensions vary, it is generally wide and deep.

The five kilometre long cave tunnels beneath nine mountains. The river course within the cave is about four kilometres and originates from a surface stream in the **Dayao Mountains**. Down part of the river, boats cruise through the cave. After exiting the cave, a small rail line takes visitors back to the entrance.

The Fengyu Cave has 10 branches. The largest chamber is 36 meters high and bristles with newly formed stalactites and stalagmites by fresh mineral deposits. One of the largest halls covers an area of over 25,000 square meters. In the main chamber a 9.8 metre stalactite only 14cms in diameter is known as the **"Diving Needle to Subdue the Sea"**.

Donglixiao Village, Shanhe Town, Lipu County, Guilin (桂林山河镇荔浦县). *www. cnfyy.cn*

Opening hours are 08.30 – 17.30 and entrance is RMB260. Buses run from Guilin and Yangshuo to Lipu County, then transfer onto a local bus to Shanhe Town.

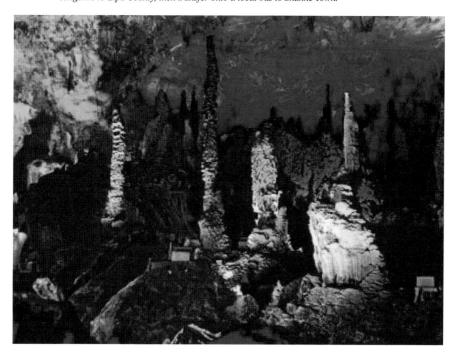

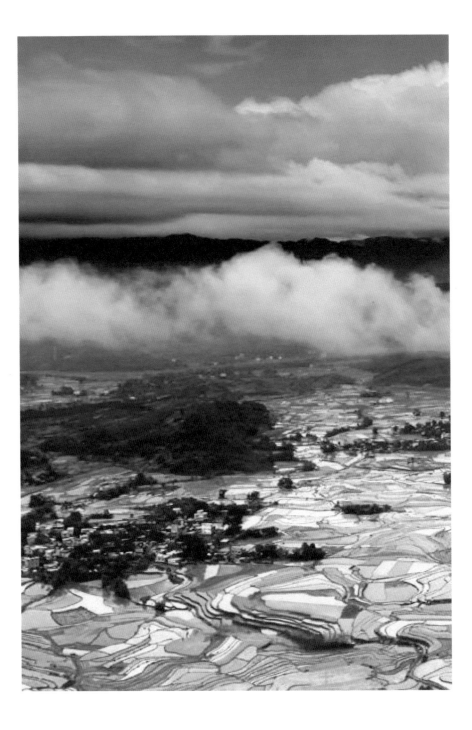

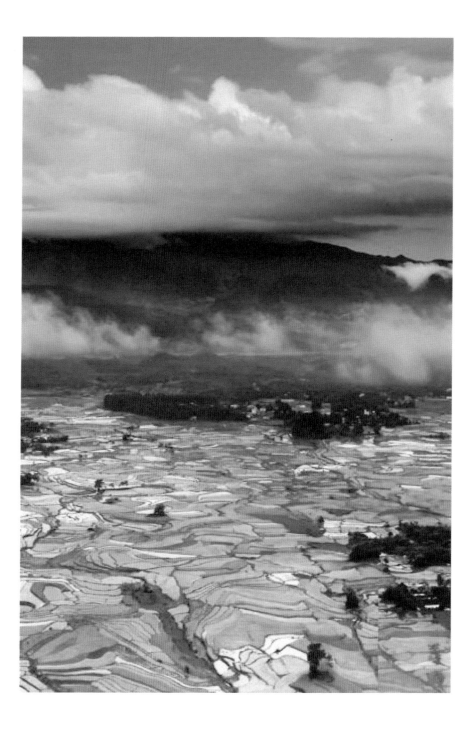

6 The Outer Counties

Guilin, Longsheng and Yangshuo are tourist towns par excellence but increasingly, travellers are exploring further afield, as new roads make the other eight counties of Guilin more accessible.

LOCAL governments are busy trying to convert their rural counties into tourist friendly locales and promote the regional highlights. At the time of writing this is still a work-in-progress. But there are remote marvels, little known gems and historic wonders, that if you've the time to spend, and enough curiosity, are well worth checking out.

Jiangtouzhou (江头洲)

In **Lingchuan County** just north of Guilin you'll find this redolent, 1000-year-old village. The village lies about two kilometres from Jiuwu Town. Most of the villagers are descendants of **Zhou Dunyi**, a famous writer, philosopher and neo-Confucianism scholar from Hunan who migrated into Guangxi during the Northern Song Dynasty; thus Zhou is the most common surname. Set before a plain of pastoral fields lined by a series of stunning karst mountains, you can see why Zhou established Jiangtouzhou in this fertile quarter. The village is characterized by a maze of narrow alleyways lined by houses mostly constructed during the Ming and Qing.

At the time of writing a large-scale, village-wide renovation was underway to turn Jiangtouzhou into a national tourist scenic spot. Certainly some of the crumbling, overgrown farmhouses need rescuing. But how sensitive the redevelopment is remains to be seen. For the time-being at least, Jiangtouzhou is a place where one can get up close and smell the history, wander cobbled paths, watch villagers wash their clothes in the river or perch on the magnificent Ming-era **Hulong Bridge**, and wax lyrical about the

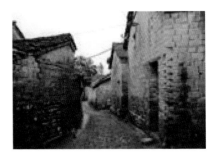

serenity of this scene, unencumbered by the trappings of mass-tourism.

A kilometre away, set in the hills is **Jinshan Temple** (金山庙) a scenic and very active Buddhist temple. It's open more to the visiting faithful than to tourists, but is worthy of a photo if you are passing by.

To get to **Jiangtouzhuang**, set out from **Guilin North Bus Station**. Take the No.302 bus, get off at Tanxia crossing(潭下路口), then take the local bus to **Jiuwu** (九屋) and walk 10 minutes to get to the village. The whole journey takes about 40mins.

Alternatively cycle north along **Zhengshan Beilu** for 1km then turn left onto Huancheng Beiyilu and take the first right. Cycle north through **Dingjiang Town** then follow a country lane for about 30 minutes (15km). At a fork in the road bare right towards **Tanxia Town** and follow signs to Jiuwu. Jiangtouzhou is down a trail just past Jiuwu.

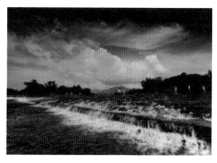

Lingqu Canal (灵渠)

Lingqu Canal, built in 214BC by the Yellow Emperor, is one of the oldest and best preserved man-made-made waterways in the world. The canal, which has a total length of 37.4km, connects the Xiang River and Li River, thus providing a crucial link between the Yangtze and Pearl River systems. The canal allowed the emperor to move troops and supplies quickly and secretly from the central heartlands of the empire, playing an important role in the unification o China. The canal, which used the most advanced technology of its time, took only 33 years to build. To this day the canal still plays an important part in water conversation, flood mitigation and irrigation in the region. Lingqu Canal is located 57km north of Guilin in Xing'an County. Visitors can admire the design and the many ancient bridges over the canal. The Hua dyke, the main feature of the channel head, is a dam in the form of the Chinese character " 人 ", meaning people. The scenery on both sides of the canal is picturesque and nearby is the bustling market town of Xing'an and the Shujie Pagoda.

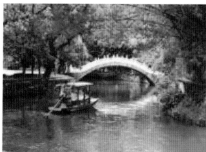

Shuangling Rd, Xing'an County, Guilin （桂林市兴安县双灵路）. Tel: 0773-621022. Admission is RMB60, RMB 30 for the tricycle car & RMB 80 for boating.

Bus route: Express buses depart every 30mins for Xing'an from Guilin Bus Station, (RMB18). After arriving at Xing'an County bus Station, take a tuk-tuk to Ling Canal (RMB 10).

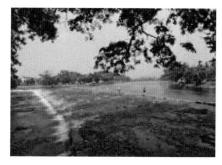

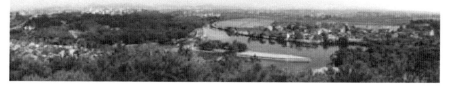

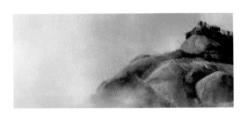

Cat Mountain (Mao'er Shan)
(猫儿山森林公园)

Direct buses from Qunzhong Road, Beiji Square in Guilin leave regularly for Cat Mountain each day from 10:30 to 15:30. The three-hour bus journey to **Xing'an County** alone makes a visit to **Mao'er Shan Nature Reserve** worthwhile, as you really encounter some bucolic scenery en route.

Before you get to the foot of the mountain you'll pass the verbosely branded **Lijiangyuan Grand Canyon**. It doesn't quite live up to the image its name conjures up but the **RMB50-70** entrance ticket will win you entrance to a stunning forested park bisected by a crashing crystalline river. Lijiangyuan is well worthy of a visit either before or after Cat Mountain, especially if you enjoy country hiking. The parks comprises six kilometres of protected land, stretching from 500 to 2000 metres above sea level. It's home to plenty of wildlife, evident in the birdsong permeating the air or the giant salamanders that make the many waterways their home. Exuding the Chinese fetish for symbolism, notable scenic spots bear names like **Dragon Well** and **Rhino Hump**.

Further up the road **Cat Mountain** dominates the scenery. Not surprising this, as it's the tallest mountain south of the Nanling Range that separates the Deep South from the rest of China. The **RMB180** ticket gets you a seat on a tour bus that takes sightseers up the nature reserve's winding mountain roads. Once you breach the cloud line the bus will occasionally pause at various scenic points so tourists can photograph the **cloud sea** (clouds perforated by mountain top islets) for which the region is famous.

The mountain is also the source of the Li, Zi and Xun rivers, and boardwalks that zigzag through the mountainside forests enable close access to these swampy wellsprings. The habitat is rich with wildlife including tree frogs and apparently black bears still dwell up here, so take care.

The bus will drop you at the **Cloud Summit Holiday Resort** and the final leg to the top has to be made on foot. On the way there are some Taoist effigies, in case you'd like to pray for a bit of good luck. There's also an interesting museum near the summit telling the story of the **Flying Tigers**, a squadron of American pilots based in Guilin and Kunming who fought the Japanese in the air during World War Two [see xxxx]. Many lost their lives in the sky battles and were never returned to their families. Remarkably, in October 1996, two Xing'an villagers, Jiang Jun and Pan Qibin, found a wreckage of a jet on Cat Mountain. It was confirmed as a B-24 bomber of the 14th US Air Force. The remains of the plane, as well as bilingual wall plaques and photographs, tell the story.

As you ascend there are several lavishly branded viewing platforms including **Immortal Sorrow Cliff** and **Buddha's Light Platform**. The highest point of 2140.6 metres is demarked by the cat's right ear (the mountain acquired its name from a rock that looks like a cat). To reach it, follow the path buoyantly labelled **Stairway to Heaven** and be rewarded with breath-taking panoramas of the surrounding countryside; that is, unless the cloud sea is at high tide.

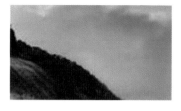

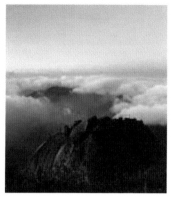

The Flying Tigers

When veteran aviator Claire Lee Chennault left the American military aged 43 due to health issues few could have his anticipated his next move. He took a three month, 3000 dollar contract in China to survey the Chinese Air Force. With the outbreak of the Sino-Japanese War, Chennault rose to become **Chiang Kai-shek's** chief air adviser, training Chinese Air Force pilots as well as conducting some scouting missions of his own. But recognising massive deficiencies in Chinese planes, with few skilled pilots to fly them, Chennault came up with the idea of the Flying Tigers, initially (and officially) known as the 1st American Volunteer Group (AVG).

Gaozhai Village, Huajiang, Xing'an County, Guilin （桂林兴安县华江乡高寨村）. *Tel:0773-6059106. Entrance is RMB160. Guilin Bus Terminal Station has a direct shuttle bus to Mao'er Shan. Otherwise you could take a bus to Xing'am, Ziyuan or Quanzhou town, then get off at the Baizhupu* （白竹铺）*stop and transfer to a shuttlebus to the mountain.*

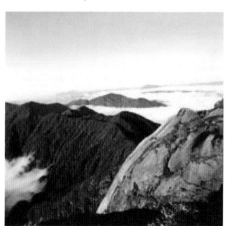

This band of winged mercenaries in their **Tomahawk IIB's** with distinctive shark face nose paint proved decidedly effective in fending off the Japanese air attacks in China. Following Chennault's radical, often unconventional tactics they destroyed 296 enemy aircraft while only losing 14 pilots. On 4 July 1942 the AVG was disbanded. With America now officially at war, it was replaced by the 23rd Fighter Group of the United States Army Air Forces, which was later absorbed into the US Fourteenth Air Force. Chennault was made a General and the 23rd FG went on to achieve similar combat success. After divorcing his first wife, Chennault married Beijing-born Chen Xiangmei who he met in Kunming. Despite continuing to support Chiang Kai-shek and the Nationalists after the war, Chennault and company are recognized by the present regime for their efforts in defending China in a time of great need. At the time of writing a **Flying Tigers Heritage Park** was under construction near Guilin city with a film biopic by acclaimed Hong Kong director John Woo also in the pipeline.

Bajiao Hamlet Scenery（八角寨）

North of **Xing'an County** you'll come upon **Ziyuan County**. The town of **Ziyuan** is a pretty and welcoming place. The government is keen to attract travellers to the corner of the county, as the newly painted houses and brightly illuminated town centre suggest. Apparently an expressway is under construction that will link Ziyuan with Guilin in under an hour.

The area around the **Zi River** has some historic sites including a gorgeous wooden **wind and rain bridge**. Along the waterfront, on Binjiang Road, you'll find some of the best eateries including **Lou Shang**, a western-style café housed in an old river watchtower. Just behind along **Danxia Road** is where most of the hotels are located. Given Ziyuan's distance from Guilin, you should plan on staying the night.

At the time of writing there is really only one natural attraction worthy enough to lure travellers away from the comfort of their Guilin bunk. The **Bajiao Gorge** three kilometres north Meixi Town, near the Hunan border, is a geo-park where you can hike about the extraordinary **danxia** rock formations.

Danxia landform is a type of petrographic geomorphology unique to South China. It earned its name from the landform first studied in neighbouring Guangdong in the 1930s around Danxia Mountain. These unique crimson formations are created in a similar way to the karst topography synonymous with Yangshuo. But reddish sandstone and conglomerates, not limestone, predominantly form danxia.

In Bajiao there are some steep and precarious hikes through the rock formations, occasionally via hanging bridges. The highest peak is 814 meters above sea level. There are three **Buddhist temples** scattered through the geo-park, two on the Guangxi side and one on the Hunan side (you can actually leave the province through the park).

As you might expect, it's the viewing points affording visitors stunning photo opportunities of the landscape, that are the principle draw.

Datuo Village, North-east of Meixi, Ziyuan County, Guilin（桂林市资源县东北部梅溪乡大坨村）. Entrance is RMB60. Take a shuttle bus from Guilin North Bus Station (RMB 30-50), then transfer at Ziyuan Bus Station to a minibus to Meixi county (RMB 5-10). From Meixi there is a tourist bus to Bajia Hamlet Scenery.

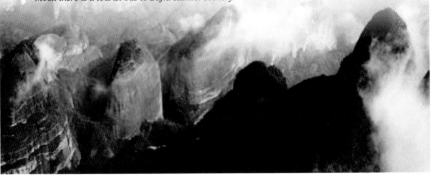

Quangzhou County (全州县)

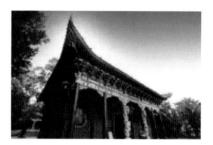

Quanzhou County on Guilin's northeastern periphery really takes you off the beaten path. Here, 129 kilometres from Guilin city, you can expect to be "helloed" at constantly, while locals might even ask if they can take your photo. That said there's not a great deal to lure tourists. The handsomely named **Heavenly Lake** is popular with local campers, but at the time of writing, the road was too bad to negotiate with anything less than a four-wheel-drive.

If you do find yourself out this way, then **Xiangshan Temple** (湘山寺) is worthy of a visit. The temple was established in 756AD by a famous Tang dynasty monk and was once considered one of the most important in southern China. It's a sizeable religious complex surrounded by verdant hills. There are hiking paths to pavilions that afford great views of Guilin's largest county. The highlight is the superb 28-metre **Miaoming Pagoda** (妙明塔) first constructed in 874AD.

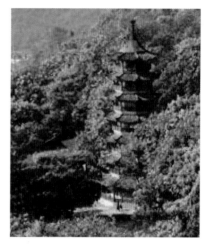

Guihuang Mid Road, Quanzhou County,Guilin (桂林市全州县桂黄中路). *Tel:0773-4812941. http://xiangshansi.fjsy.net*
It's RMB10 for locals to enter and RMB60 for outsiders.

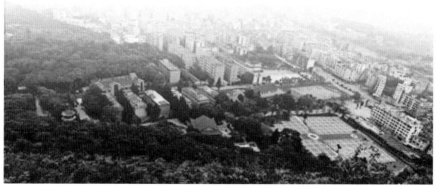

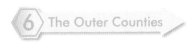

Yao Autonomous County of Gongcheng
(恭城瑶族自治县)

Superficially at least, Gongcheng is an average, if pleasant enough river locale most famously associated with the wide variety of fruits produced here. The best time to arrive is the autumn harvest season when the persimmon festival is held. Now its on the Guizhou to Guangzhou high-speed rail line, Yangshuo's sister county is far easier to reach, and has some real historic treats to take in.

In the town centre head to **Guyang Street** (古样街), a rustic old street comprising wood and stone houses that offer an interesting insight into traditional Gongcheng life before the wrecking ball. At the head of the street you'll find two architectural marvels to explore. The **Zhouwei Temple** was built in the year 1478 in memory of Zhou Wei a prominent Song dynasty administrator famous for beseeching the emperor to lower exorbitant taxes and set up schools to provide education opportunities for his people. Next door, the **Hunan Assembly Hall** is the best preserved of four regional Qing dynasty temples. It now houses a Communist Party anti-corruption exhibition.

A little out of town there are more Ming temples to explore, the **Wen Miao** and **Wu Miao**. The former is one of the best-preserved Confucian temples in the region, the later was built in 1603 to venerate the famous Three Kingdoms general **Guan Yu**. Both are RMB40 to enter. The newly constructed **Pangwan Temple**, replete with park like gardens, is situated just between these historic halls and offers a pleasant enough stroll.

High speed trains run regularly from Guilin North Station to Gongcheng Station between 07.47 and 21.01. The journey takes about 45 minutes and costs RMB30 in second-class and RMB37.5 for first-class.

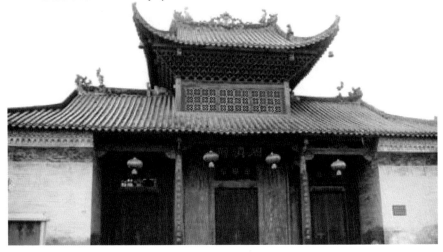

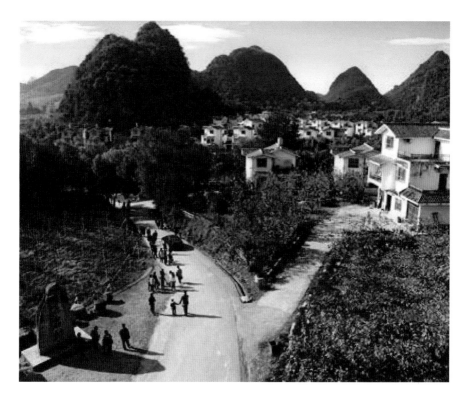

Hongyan Village (红岩村)

14 kilometres down the road in the direction of Yangshuo you'll find **Hongyan Village**, a stunning yet strange place. Superficially it's an idyllic locale, where white washed villas overlook tidy streets lined by persimmon trees; Yangshuo meets an affluent American suburb. Persimmons are the local speciality, and there's a persimmon festival held each autumn to commemorate the harvest. Local Yao folk hawk all kinds of persimmon-derived treats to visitors. The pretty, made-to-look old **Fengyu Bridge** traverses the **Pingyang River** where locals offer bamboo raft rides. And hundreds of farmhouses have been converted into guesthouses and restaurants.

What is weird about this too-good-to-be-true locale is that it welds the concept of a model village commonly associated with communism with the kind of commercial resort one might associate with capitalism in, say, Florida. According to the tourist blurb, **Hongyan Village Ecological Scenic Area** was actually "constructed" in 2002 to offer sightseers a vision of a "rustic farming experience". In a region where rural poverty is rife, especially in ethnic minority areas, Hongyan presents an idealised vision of life in rural Guangxi. But if you're happy to buy into the myth, its worthy of a day or so away from Yangshuo, as the scenery is stunning, the village quaint and accommodation comfortable.

Lipu Pagoda (荔浦塔)

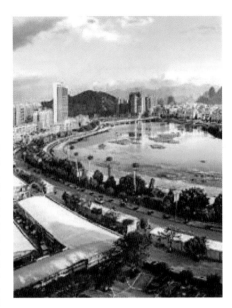

South of Yangshuo, Lipu is a typical river town administering a largely rural county. It certainly hasn't been "opened-up" to tourism in any meaningful way, which is a shame because it has a few marvellous old buildings that are badly in need of repair. That said, if you're a history buff or interested in viewing something of ancient China before it's been glossed with paint and fitted with a toll gate, cycle or bus down to Lipu and head for Baota Lane (宝塔巷). This old quarter, hidden from town by a façade of new shops and houses, is an example of a China fast disappearing from view. Cobbled streets, wood and stone building and a dilapidated Taoist hall muster some serious ambience. But it is the fairy-tale **Lipu Pagoda**, a seven-story tower in the midst of this mottled old area that is the must-take Lipu photograph.

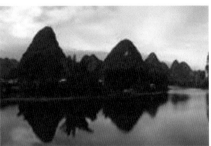

Get a shuttlebus from Yangshuo Bus Terminal Station Shima South substation. Buses run every 10mins and the one hour journey costs RMB 7. Most of the buses to Lipu will pass Silver Water Cave (see pxxx).

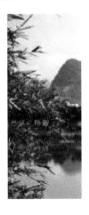

Red Army Sites

Throughout China's war blasted years after the fall of the Qing dynasty in 1911, the Communist Party (CCP) had initially cooperated with the Nationalists (KMT) led by **Chiang Kai-shek** but after the **April 12th Incident** in 1923 – a massacre of Communists in Shanghai ordered by Chiang – the CCP retreated to rural soviets mostly in the South. When the KMT surrounded the Jiangxi Soviet in 1933, the CCP had no choice but to breakout and make an epic retreat, now known as the **Long March**, which began in 1934. As they passed through Guilin, the Communists fought skirmishes and recruited locals to the socialist cause.

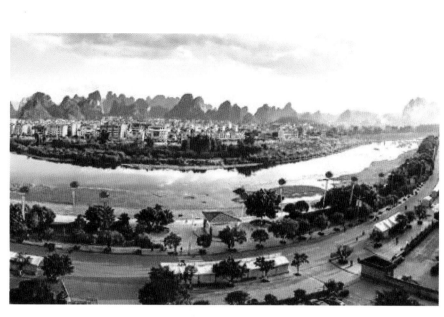

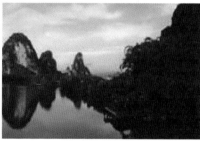

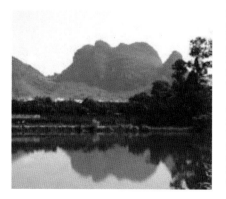

Most local events concerning the CCP, big and small, are now commemorated with several **Red Army Sites** in the region. These include bridges and notable buildings, as well as revolutionary martyrs' monuments.

Curiously, Guilin enjoyed something of a cultural and economic boom in the late-30s as manufacturing relocated there and intellectuals fled south. Guo Moruo, Liu Yazi and He Xiangning were among those who made a home in the city. The Eighth Route Army's Guilin Office, the former site of which is just above the city, was a beneficiary of Guangxi's relative independence. These offices had been established by the CCP in a number of cities after the united front agreement with the Nationalists. As the Japanese threatened, the Communists were permitted to move to Guilin.

The Japanese eventually overran Guangxi's capital during **Operation Ichigo** in 1944. Much life was lost and tragedy ensued in the chaos of the evacuation. But a guerrilla campaign led by some valiant Guangxi locals did afford the Japanese some bother. Both Nationalist and Communist accounts claim the south Guangxi guerrillas as theirs.

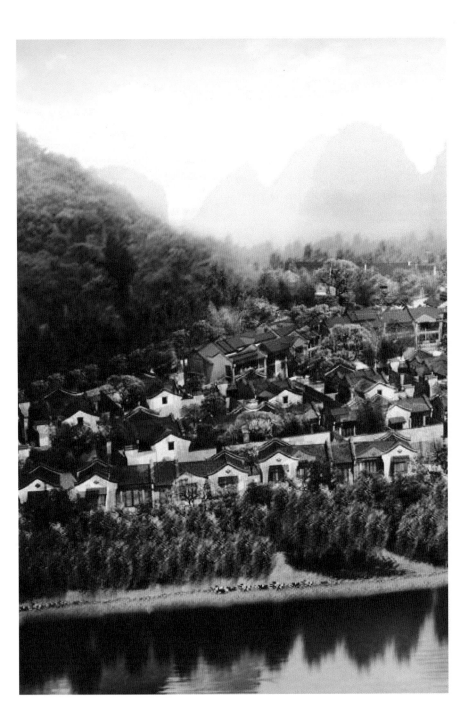

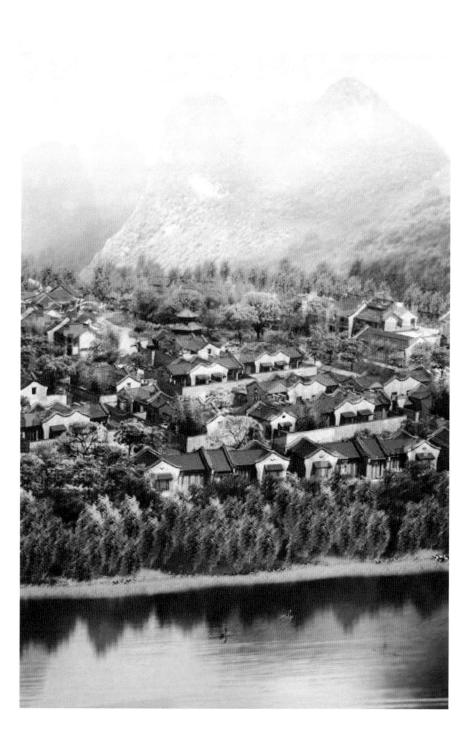

7 Practical Information

Accommodation

Guilin

GUILIN, a veritable diamond in China's tourism tiara, sparkles with high-end hostelries including the lake-side VIP haunt **Rong Hu Hotel**, the aptly named, cascading **Waterfall Hotel**, and the well-heeled but distant **Shangri-La**.

Many visitors choose to base themselves around the **Zhengyang Pedestrian Street** whose cluster of eateries, bars and hotels make it a solid place to orientate your travels from. Just off **Zhengyang Pedestrian Street** along **Renmin Road** you'll find two quality accommodation options; **Guilin Hostel** for backpackers and **Sheraton Guilin Hotel** for the executive class. Along adjacent **Binjiang Road**, which overlooks the Li River, there are also quite a few hotels to choose from.

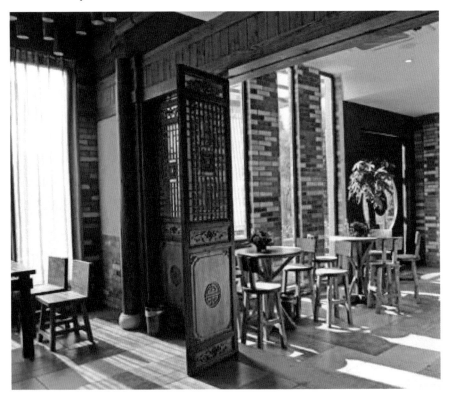

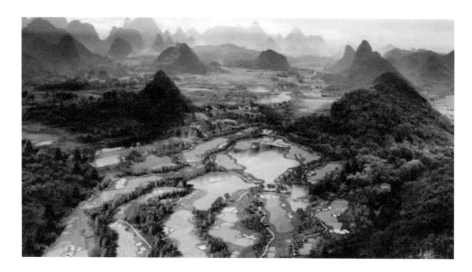

Yangshuo and Around

With more than **10,000 beds** available each night across Yangshuo County's 250 or more registered hotels, accommodation options are plentiful. If you are only in town for a few days, it would be advisable to choose somewhere in or around West Street with its plethora of tour-booking agents/bike rental/restaurants and bars. The accommodation here ranges from backpacker dives like **Monkey Jane's** to the charming old town architecture of West Street's finest establishment, the **Hongfu Palace Hotel**. If West Street feels crowded and pricey then the still central area around **Chengbei Road** has some of the better hotels that combine cheapness and quality of stay. The most famous establishment on this street is **Lisa's**.

For those that have a little longer in Yangshuo, we suggest you look into one of the excellent countryside options. To the north of the city, roads meander along with the Li River through charming deserted hamlets surrounded by paddy fields. **Trippers Carpe Diem** provides backpacker amenities at good rates. A popular area out west is along the **Yulong River** –well-located for cycling the Moon Hill route, exploring the old townships of **Xiatang** and **Jiuxian** and rafting the **Yulong**. A top choice here would be The **Giggling Tree**, a charming Dutch-owned establishment comprised of a selection of gentrified farm-shacks linked into a courtyard. For those seeking a taste of old-China charm, Jiuxian's **Secret Garden** and **Xiatang's Old Manor House** fit the bill. To the east and across the Li River bridge, **Dahutong Hotel** is incredibly peaceful and offers a great option for those hoping to completely escape the tourist vibe. Sitting on Ten Li Picture Gallery tourist trail, just south of Yangshuo is the **Gallery Inn**, which caters to artists.

Price for a standard double room in peak season
¥ = less than RMB200
¥¥ = RMB200-500
¥¥¥ RMB500+

Guilin Hotels

Shangri-La Hotel 香格里拉大酒店

111 Huancheng North Second Rd, Qixing District, Guilin

桂林七星区环城二路 111 号

Tel:0773-2698888

Designed by a Hong Kong architect in a riverside garden setting, the Guilin Shangri-La is a hike from downtown, but offers all you expect of this premium hotel brand, including spacious suites, health club and spa, swanky eateries like the Shang Palace, and even a few extras like a BBQ terrace and a Bread Bar.

Sheraton Guilin Hotel 桂林喜来登饭店

15 Bin Jiang Road, Xiufeng District, Guilin

桂林秀峰区滨江路 15 号

Tel: 86 773 282 5588

Website: sheraton.com/guilin

Sheraton Guilin Hotel is ideally located on the west bank of the Li River as well as situated right in central city featuring Roman style lobby, sightseeing lift and interior garden. The Zhengyang walking street and the most popular snack street are only steps away. The hotel's geographical location is richly endowed by nature with the beautiful Elephant Trunk and Fubo Hill around.

Guilin Lijiang Waterfall Hotel 漓江大瀑布饭店

1 Shahu North Rd, Xiufeng District

桂林市秀峰区杉湖北路 1 号

Tel: 0773-2822801

A Guilin landmark whose guest rooms offer alluring views of the Sun and Moon Twin Pagodas. The real attraction is the man-made waterfall - the largest in the world - cascading down the outside.

Royal Garden Hotel 桂林帝苑酒店

186-1, Linjiang Road, Qixing District, Guilin

桂林七星区临江路 186-1 号

Tel:0773-5688888

On the banks of the Li, opposite Fubo Hill and Diecai Hill, this superior hotel enjoys a pastoral ambience of water and hill, and good river views.

Rong Hu Hotel 榕湖饭店

16 Ronghu North Rd, Xiufeng District, Guilin

桂林秀峰区榕湖北路 16 号

Tel:0773-2895173

A garden hotel on the west bank of the picturesque Rong Lake which is a favourite with visiting VIPs. The hotel hosts displays of ancient inscriptions and seals.

Riverview Hotel 好地方江景酒店

17 Binjiang Rd, Xiufeng District, Guilin

桂林市秀峰区滨江路 17 号

Tel:0773-2834666

A small hotel facing the river on Binjiang Road, near the Zhengyang Pedestrian Street. The clean, average-sized rooms offer river views and hot showers.

Mingcheng Hotel 名城大酒店

6 Zhengyang Rd, Xiufeng District, Guilin
桂林 秀峰区正阳路 6 号
Tel: 0773-2882008
This low-key Chinese-style hotel on the corner of Renmin Rd and the Zhengyang Pedestrian Street is a classic of its type right down to the old-style lobby, faded carpets, and slight damp, but it puts you in the centre of things.

Old Place Youth Hostel
老地方青年旅舍

2 Yiwu Rd, Xiufeng District, Guilin
桂林市秀峰区翼武路 2 号（医务旅与桥家具会
址）Tel: 0773-2813598
Sat on a sleepy stretch of the river front, this new kid in the Hostelling International family offers travelers a cozy lounge, helpful English speakers, bacon and egg breakfasts, and many tourist services.

Guilin Central Hostel
火车青年旅舍

3 Renmin Rd, Xiangshan District (Near Zhengyang Walking Street, diagonally opposite the Sheraton Hotel) 桂林市象山区人民路 3 号
Tel: 0773-2819939
One of Guilin's stand-out hostels due to large rooms, a good café, friendly staff, helpful tourist info., and a handy location by the Zhengyang Pedestrian Street and Li River.

Yangshuo Hotels

Monkey Jane's 齐饲客栈

No.24 Lianfeng Mid Rd, West Street, Yangshuo County. 阳朔县西街莲峰中路 24 号 Tel: 0773-8814086
This Yangshuo institution behind West Street has basic rooms but the excellent rooftop bar draws the backpacker/ English teacher crowd.

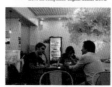

Da Huwai 大户外

5-1,Mushanzha,Dongling Rd, Yangshuo County
桂林阳朔东岭木山榨 5-1 号
Tel: 0773-8822772
Courtyard hotel in the countryside on the road to Fuli, which under the tutelage of its idealistic owner Simon is far more than a guesthouse but a centre for international exchange where guests can learn about Chinese culture, language and cooking.

Giggling Tree 格格树度假酒店

Aishanmen Village, Yangshuo County
阳朔县埋山门村 Tel:13661266754
Outstanding rustic hotel near some of the best Yulong River cycling routes. The Dutch owners have lovingly created characterful guest rooms inside converted county houses. Al fresco dining in the courtyard is another draw and the hotel also offers good tourist maps and bike hire.

Secret Garden 秘密花园

Jiuxian Village, Yangshuo County
阳朔旧县茶村门 Tel:0773-8771932
Sprawling up the hill behind Jiuxian Village, this impressive hotel makes creative use of terraces, gardens, and mountain paths. The converted village properties house beautiful en-suite rooms.

Trippers Carpe Diem
阳朔山景假日酒店

35 Shiban Bridge, Yangshuo County
阳朔石板桥 35 号 Tel:0773-8822533
Trippers Carpe Diem dominates the accommodation offerings in this popular area and the Belgium owners provide backpacker amenities at good rates.

Green Lotus Hotel 绿莲江景大酒店

No.1 Guanlian Rd, Yangshuo County, Guilin 桂林阳朔观莲路 1 号 Tel:0773-8886666
A Hilton style behemoth just east of town, it was said that charismatic former president Jiang Zemin insisted on staying here every time when he came to Yangshuo.

Banyan Tree 阳朔悦榕庄

No.168 Zhengdong Street, Fuli Town, Yangshuo County 富村镇正东街 168 号（阳朔福利镇东去）Tel:0773-3226888
Currently the premium option in Yangshuo's countryside, Banyan offers villa style accommodation in an environment exquisitely designed in accordance with fengshui principles. In addition to its facilities such as swimming pool and spa, the hotel supports cultural activities in surrounding villages.

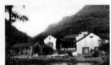

Yunhouse Boutique Hotel
阳朔云庐精品酒店

Yangjia Village, Xingping, Yangshuo County
阳朔兴坪杨家村 Tel: 0773-8703008
Another high-end – and high priced – resort hotel in the Yangshuo countryside, with beautifully appointed rooms and courtyard dining, but no swimming pool or spa.

Kaiyue Hotel

Old Street, Xingping
Small hotel located slap in the middle of Xingping which offers rooms with wifi, partitioned showers and balconies overlooking the Old Street. Access to the guest rooms on the second floor is through a gift shop.

Old Place Youth Hostel

Xingping
Turn right from exit of the old city
Xinping's best hostel is located just outside Old Street. Upstairs from a comfortable lobby fitted with bookshelves, bar, and sofas, are clean rooms with balconies. The hotel offers continental and American breakfasts, and next door there is an attractive book bar/café.

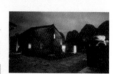

Yangshuo Old Manor House
阳朔老宅院

Xia Tang Village, Yangshuo County, Guilin City 阳朔县夏棠村 Tel: 0773-8825900
Email: oldmanor-house@hotmail.com
www.old-manor-house.com
This new hotel at peaceful Xiatang Village near the Yulong River is based around beautifully reconstructed 400 year old village houses, which preserve many original features. The German owner will no doubt tell you the fascinating story of the reconstruction, while serving you food and beverages.

Gallery Inn 画廊别院

阳朔县 10 里画廊橙兔旅舍斜对面，画廊别院对面：
Tel: 18177317171 / 0773-8885078
This artists' retreat a kilometre or so south of Yangshuo is a real hidden treasure. Tucked away just off the main drag that leads to Moon Hill, rooms encircle a private lake while stunning karst outcroppings bear down over the hotel. If you're really looking to get away from it all and enjoy the scenery, Gallery Inn is a great mid-range option.

128

Budgeting

Guilin is cheaper than China's most developed cities such as Beijing and Shanghai but admission to some attractions can be pricey. Splurge on white water rafting, or the **Impressions: Liu Sanjie** show, and costs can mount up. If you stay in a cheap guesthouse on Yangshuo's **West Street**, get around by bike and eat in local restaurants, then an average budget of RMB400/day should be enough. If you prefer to book a business class hotel, and travel in style by private car then you could easily blow upwards of RMB1000/day. However, hotel prices are around 30% lower outside the peak season roughly from May to October. In the end it should be possible for those of all budgets to enjoy a rewarding trip. Guideline costs in Chinese Yuan (CNY) are as follows:

Main course at a budget/moderate restaurant: RMB40/RMB80
Double room in a budget/business class hotel: RMB120/RMB300
English boat tourist ticket from Guilin to Yangshuo: RMB420
Bike/motorbike hire one day (Yangshuo): RMB30/80
Private car hire for one day: RMB400-500
Full price admission to Elephant Trunk Park/ Yangshuo: Impressions show: RMB75/280

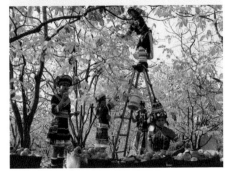

Festivals

Chinese National Festivals (2016, 2017,2018)

Chinese New Year (Feb 08, Jan28, Feb16)
Lantern Festival (Feb 22, Feb 11, March 2)
Qing Ming (Tomb Sweeping) Festival (April 4, April 4, April 5)
Dragon Boat Festival
(June 9, May 30, Jun 18)
Mid-Autumn Festival
(Sept 16,Oct 2, Sep 25)

Local Festivals

Guilin also has a number of interesting local festivals of ancient or modern provenance.

Yangshuo Rock Climbing Festival (阳朔攀岩节)

This event, launched in 2008, has become increasingly popular, with Yangshuo's scenery and reputation as China's climbing hotspot drawing foreign famous climbers and local enthusiasts. *The Rock Climbing festival is held at end of October or beginning of November. Check the website, www.rockclimbing.cn.*

Ghost Festival (鬼节)

The 'Ghost Festival', also known as the 'Mid-July Festival', is a popular ancestor worship festival with a history of several hundred years. At this time, locals 'invite' the spirits of their ancestors back home to receive their offerings before escorting them back to Soul Mountain. The festival is also associated with eating 'dog tongue cake'(狗舌粑). *Festival dates are based on the lunar calendar; it usually falls in early or mid August.*

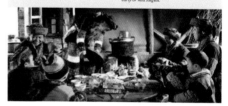

Zhuang Folk Music Festival
（壮族会山歌）

On the evening of the mid-autumn festival, under the full moon, Zhuang villages float with the melodious sound of flute music and singing. This is essentially a Zhuang 'Valentine's Day', with young people singing songs as a way to identify the right partner before declaring their feelings in song. Many Zhuang people, it is said, meet their matches this way. Moon Hill in Yangshuo is a popular place to gather and sing. *The Mid-Autumn Festival usually falls in the first half of September.*

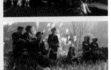

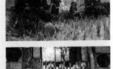

Yangshuo Fishing Boat Light Festival
（阳朔渔火节）

Along the Li River on this festival day, the cormorant fishing people line up their boats, and their birds, in the middle of the river to fish together by lamplight, a memorable sight. *The festival is usually held every October.*

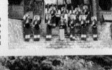

Yangshuo Land God Festival
（阳朔社日）

This popular festival is ostensibly about making offerings to the Land God Buddha but is really an opportunity for Yangshuo men to have a get-together. The festival emphasizes comradeship and mutual assistance.

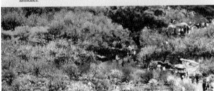

Local Markets

Despite the growth of tourism, Yangshuo remains a traditional, agricultural place. Many of the surrounding local towns and villages hold lively markets throughout the month. Nowadays, as well as local produce and handicrafts, you'll see mass-produced garments being hawked, but that doesn't diminish the general ambience of an old time bazaar. Market days are especially good to visit if you're cycling around the area. Check the dates below and see if any match yours.

1, 4, 7, 14, 17, 21, 24 and 27 are market days for Yangdi, Maling and Baisha.

2, 5, 8, 12, 15, 18, 22, 25 and 28 are dates for Fuli and Putao.

3, 6, 9, 13, 16, 19, 23, 26 and 29 are dates for Yangshuo, Xingping, Puyi and Jinbao.

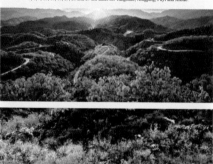

Food

Guilin, with its rich pastoral lands, produces a lot of great food. That said many tourists come to Guilin to try two things: **Beer fish** and **Rice noodles**.

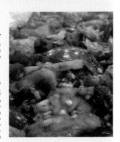

Beer Fish (啤酒鱼)

This delicious concoction is made from a mixture of the local **Li Spring Beer**, mild chili peppers and the catch of the day. Most restaurants stock fish in tanks so usually you can choose your fish. Each fish is priced on the menu by the jin (500g) so be careful not to misunderstand the price, and be sure to make sure that the fish you select is the fish that you get served as it is common for certain restaurants to switch fishes.

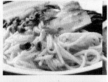

Guilin Rice Noodles (米粉)

While it is typical for towns across China to serve their own variation of a similar fish dish, **Guilin Rice Noodles** is truly authentic. Made from locally grown rice that is pressed and moulded into noodles, it has a delicious vermicelli style texture – typically each restaurant offers their own special 'gravy' and it is up to the client to add in their choice spices, chives, chili peppers and other bits from a selection of pots around the restaurant.

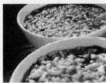

Li River Crayfish (小龙虾)

Cooked fresh from the basket and served in a deliciously well-spiced sauce, Li River crayfish are one of the highlights of the local cuisine. In Yangshuo, usually the freshest of these are served to the southeast of West Street, on **Pantao Road** (蟠桃路).

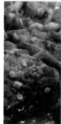
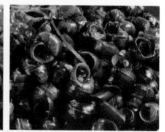

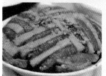
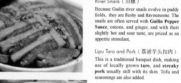

River Snails（田螺）

Because Guilin river snails evolve in paddy fields, they are fleshy and flavoursome. The snails are often served with **Guilin Pepper Sauce**, onions, and ginger, and with their slightly hot and sour taste, are prized as an appetite stimulant.

Lipu Taro and Pork（荔浦芋头扣肉）

This is a traditional banquet dish, making use of locally grown **taro**, and **streaky pork** usually still with its skin. Tofu and seasonings are also added.

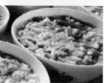

Yao Oil Tea（油茶）

Yao Oil Tea is prepared by frying tea leaves, usually in peanut oil, with garlic, salt, ginger, chili, and possibly other ingredients. Water is then added and the mixture boiled. The tea is believed by the **Yao people** of Gongcheng County to enhance the immune system and keep them warm in winter.

134

Getting Around

Bike Rental

Cycling is a great option for getting around Guilin City, Yangshuo and the surrounding countryside.

Guilin

Guilin City runs a well-organized **city bike** service. The bikes are available at 106 rental kiosks around the city, including a convenient one on the river front close to the Elephant Trunk Park. Daily rental is RMB30 with a RMB200 deposit and service hours are from 07.00 – 21.00 in peak season, 07.00 – 19.00 off-peak.

Meanwhile **bikes** can also be hired at similar cost from guesthouses like the Central Hostel on Renmin Road.

Yangshuo

There are bike rental outlets all over Yangshuo The going rate is RMB10/ hour or RMB30/day in the peak season. A RMB200 deposit is normally required, and you will need to show ID.

One of the most popular areas for cycling is around the Yulong River, where you will again find **many bike rental stations**. If you take to the Yulong waters on a bamboo raft, your bike can often be transported to meet you at the other end.

Experienced cyclists with an appetite for endurance may like to try more ambitious routes, such as the hard bike to Xingping (see p92). In this case it could make sense to rent from somewhere like the **Bike Asia** shop on Guihua Road, which also provides maps and guides.

Boat

Hopping on one of the many **tourist boat services** traversing the Li and Yulong rivers is a great way to experience the Guilin region's scenic beauty. The classic Li River cruise is the 4-4.5hr service from **Guilin to Yangshuo**. The boats come with guides (for details see p. xxxx). Prices are about RMB245-260 for Chinese guide boats, including a bus to the ferry, and RMB420 for the English ones (see page 67).

It is also possible to take **motorized bamboo boats** down the Li from Yangdi to the Nine Horse Picture Hill or on to Xingping. (See page 68). The cost is RMB120 to Yangdi and an extra RMB30 to continue to Xingping. Bamboo boat services are also a way to explore riverside villages around Yangshuo, such as the Fishing Village.

Bamboo rafting on the Yulong River is popular, although it is not possible to commandeer a boat independently. For details (see page 88).

Buses

Guilin City Buses

Guilin is a relatively small city with the town centre negotiable on foot. The city area has a well-developed **bus network** and a new fleet of buses. The flat fare for normal buses is RMB1.

There are also several convenient **tourist city bus** routes, including the #30 and #266, which both run along East Jiefang Road nearby the Zhengyang Pedestrian Street. #30 will take you to Seven Star Park. The air conditioned tourist buses are a bargain at RMB2.

Getting Around the Guilin Scenic Area By Bus

Services to Yangshuo (RMB20/2 hours) depart from **Guilin Bus Terminus** (see 'Getting There') conveniently located downtown, as well as from Guilin Train Station. The service to Xingping (RMB20/2.5 hours) passes through Yangshuo. Meanwhile buses to the Yangdi Ferry also depart from Guilin Bus Terminus and take one hour.

Guilin's newest bus station, **Guilin Qintan** offers services to western counties of the greater Guilin area such as Lingui, Xuanzhou, Sanjiang and Longsheng. Local bus routes 1, 2, 12, 23, 81, 88, 91, 99 and 301 will all take you there.

Guilin Qintan Bus Station

（琴潭汽车站）

31 Cuizhu Rd, Xiangshan District, Guilin（桂林市象山区翠竹路 31 号，满泉啤酒厂附近．）
Tel:0773-3832703

Guilin North Bus Station mainly services counties in **north Guilin** including Xing'an, Quanzhou, Guanyang and Ziyuan County. Local buses 2, 32 and 85 will get you to the bus station. Most services run from 07.30-18.30.

Guilin North Bus Station

（桂林汽车运北站）

76 Beichen Rd, Diecai District, Guilin（桂林市叠彩区北辰路 76 号）
Tel:0773-3832703

Yangshuo

Yangshuo has **two bus stations**, connected by the #5 bus route. From the end of **West Street** you could take a motorcycle taxi to either station for about RMB5.

The **Dacunmen North Bus Station** offers services to important tourist locations like Guilin City, Yangdi ferry and the Yulong River. Shuttles to Guilin depart every 15 minutes from 06.30-21.20.

Yangshuo Dacunmen North Bus Station

（阳朔汽车客运站大村门北分站）

280 Jiangjiun Rd（阳朔县大村门开发区将军路 280 号）
Meanwhile the **Yangshuo Shima South Bus Station** services destinations like Huangyao Town and Xingping.

Yangshuo Shima South Bus Station

（阳朔汽车客运站石马南分站）．

Located inside the Department of Agricultural Mechanization, Yangshuo（阳朔县农业机械化管理局大院内）．

Motorbikes/ Electric Bikes.

Motorbikes and electric bikes are also available around Yangshuo, from many of the same places renting bikes. The extra power can be useful if you are travelling to further afield places like Xingping. The daily rental charge is around RMB80 for a motorbike, including petrol, and RMB50 for an electric bike.

Taxis

Guilin

Guilin taxis are both cheap and fairly plentiful. The flag drop is **RMB7** for the first 2km, although outside of the city centre, drivers will often prefer to negotiate a fare rather than use the metre. At the train station there are a lot of unlicensed taxis, so proceed with caution.

Yangshuo

There is little need for taxis in downtown Yangshuo, although the **motorcycle taxis** at the north end of West Street do a steady trade (RMB5 most local trips.) Regular taxis, usually Santanas, are of most use for generally off-metre trips into the surrounding countryside. For the run from downtown Yangshuo to the **Yulong River**, expect to pay about RMB30.

Getting There

Plane

The Guilin scenic area is served by **Guilin Liangjiang International Airport**, 28km from downtown Guilin. More than 60 international airlines connect Guilin with 30 international cities, including Hong Kong and Singapore. Meanwhile a network of 48 domestic routes links Guilin to Chinese cities like Beijing, Shanghai and Guangzhou. A direct flight from Beijing to Guilin takes about two point five hours, and two hours from Shanghai to Guilin.

Guilin Airport (IATA: GLN) is located 28km from downtown. **Shuttle buses** run from 6am to 9pm between the airport and the Minhang Building (民航大厦) in downtown Guilin. The forty minute shuttle service costs RMB20. By taxi, the ride should cost about RMB80. Meanwhile the shuttle bus service between Guilin Airport and Yangshuo costs RMB50 and takes 1.5hours.

Yanshuo to Airport Schedule

Guilin Airport to Yangshuo: 09:30、 11:30、 13:30、 15:30、 17:00、 18:30、 20:00、 22:30
Yangshuo Bus Station to Guilin

Airport: 08:00、 10:00、 12:00、 13:30、 15:30、 17:30、 19:30、 20:30

Guilin Liangjiang International Airport (桂林两江国际机场). Tel : 0773 - 2845114 ; 0773 - 2845733;0773-2845359
www.airport-gl.com.cn/

Train

Guilin has two train stations. Most high-speed trains arrive at **Guilin North Station**, a 20-30 min taxi ride from downtown. High-speed rail is for many an excellent way to arrive in Guilin. From Guangzhou South Station there are 32 daily services between 07.23 and 20.00, with a journey time of about three hours. Tickets cost around RMB137/2nd class & RMB165/1st class seat.

From Shenzhen, the nearest mainland city to Hong Kong, there are three services a day and the journey takes about three hours and forty-five minutes. Departing from Shenzhen North Station, the journeys take 3.5hours and cost RMB212/2nd Class & RMB265/1st class. Guilin is also connected via China's burgeoning **high-speed train network** with other destinations like Hezhou and the Guangxi provincial capital of Nanning.

Tickets for high speed rail services can be bought at **Guilin travel agents** and hotels downtown.

Guilin North Train Station

(桂林火车北站).

Beichen Rd, Diecai District, Guilin (桂林叠彩区北辰路). Tel: 0773-2162222. Meanwhile Guilin Station downtown is the hub for **regular train services** travelling between Guilin and destinations such as Beijing, Zhengzhou and Guizhou. Shuttle buses to Yangshuo leave directly from Guilin Train Station (RMB20/2 hours).

Guilin Train Station

（桂林火车站）.

39 Zhongshan South Rd, Xiangshan District, Guilin (桂林市象山区中山路 39 号). Tel: 0773-2164842.
As of Spring 2016 a new **Yangshuo** high speed rail station was expected to open, actually located nearer to Xingping.
Meanwhile, if you are in Yangshuo, tickets for Guilin trains can be bought at the **Yangshuo Railway Ticket Agency** inside the reception of the Pengyuan Hotel on Chengzhong Road.

Yangshuo Railway Ticket Agency
Pengyuan Hotel, 2 Chengzhong Rd, Yangshuo (阳朔城中路 2 号鹏源酒店 前台（麦当劳旁）)
Office Hours: 09:00-12:00, 14:00-16:30.

Bus

Guilin City has three main bus stations but most long-distance services depart from **Guilin Bus Terminus** (桂林汽车总站) downtown. Local buses 100, 10, 11 and 22 will take you there. There are long-distance routes to destinations in neighbouring provinces like Hunan and Guangdong, including regular **overnight services** to Shenzhen (8 hours). Other popular destinations include the provincial capital of Nanning (4.5 hours,) and sleeper services to cities like Wuzhou, Beihai and Qinzhou.

Guilin Bus Terminus

（桂林汽车总站）.

65 Zhongshan South Rd, Xiangshan District, Guilin (桂林市象山区中山 南路 65 号). Tel: 0773-3822153/0773-3862358.
Long-distance services to and from Yangshuo's two bus stations (see 'Getting Around') generally pass through Guilin.

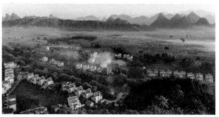

Local Products

A colourful range of local **agricultural** and **craft** products are available at markets and shops around Guilin and Yangshuo, and make good souvenirs and curiosities.

Agricultural Products (农产品)

A number of shops along Guilin's **Zhengyang Pedestrian Street**, and Yanshuo's West Street, sell products based on the area's symbol, the ubiquitous **Guihua** (Osamthumus). Guihua products include various forms of cakes and biscuits, as well as tea and wind. They are often very cheap because of being so ubquitious.

Osmanthus Cake(桂花糕)

Guilin Osmanthus Cake is a local snack of long tradition and well deserved reputation. It is flavoursome if crumbly delicacy comes in many forms.

Guihua Wine (桂花酒)

Sweet and vaguely medicinal, with a long history of local production, this refreshing tipple is supposed to **aid digestion** and blood circulation. The price of a bottle ranges from RMB18-100 depending on strength and age, with the most valued having been aged for about ten years. A 52 degrees proof version sells for about RMB80.

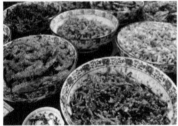

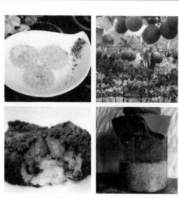

Red Pepper Paste (辣椒酱)

A famous Guilin product across China, the red pepper paste has a piquant but mellow and rich **oily flavor**. It is often eaten together with rice or bread and is also used as seasoning.

Luohan Gourds (罗汉果)

This locally grown gourd is used in **Chinese medicine** to cool and relieve congestion. After peeling open the skin it releases a sweet scent.

Fermented Bean Curd (腐乳)

Also known as '**Chinese cheese**', fermented bean curd has a sweet milky flavor which is often used to enhance the flavor of Chinese dishes. Great care is lavished on the production of this **nutritious delicacy**, with the bean curd being pummeled, filtered and pressed dry until it is a yellow orange colour of transparent lustre.

Craft Products

Many famous Guilin craft products such as **Zhuang Embroidered Balls** and **Miao Embroidery** are expressions of the region's **minority cultures**. Guilin landscapes also make for popular mementos. A good place to discover local crafts is again West Street and the area around the Zhengyang Pedestrian Street. There you will also find many generic 'China-style' souvenirs like silk scarves, jade and wood carvings, and paper umbrellas and fans.

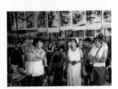

Landscape Paintings (山水画)

As a symbolic subject of Chinese landscape art since the 1940s, Guilin is a draw for artists. Copies and prints of Guilin **scenery paintings** or drawings make appropriate and popular souvenirs.

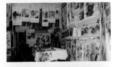

Painted paper fans (纸扇)

Colourful Guilin painted fans can be made with either **paper** or **silk**, and have a bamboo stem. Patterns include birds, insects, flowers and girls in traditional Chinese garb. The fans are available in Yangshuo and in a workshop in **Fuli Ancient Town** you can try your hand at making them.

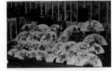

Painted paper umbrellas (纸伞)

Guillin has a **400 year history** of making paper umbrellas, which come in a variety of style and also make for attractive souvenir gifts.

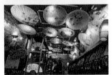

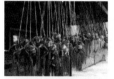

Zhuang Embroidered Balls
（壮族绣球）

These attractive embroidered silk balls were used in traditional **courtship rituals**, with Zhuang women presenting them to their beaus. The patterns indicate the connection of 12 petals, or months, which each one having a symbol such as plum blossom, bamboo, or dragon. There are three layers to the balls, all woven. The weave of **hand-woven balls** is flatter and looser.

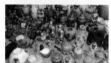

Miao Embroidery（苗绣）

Miao embroidery uses **five colour threads** and features **geometric patterns** and only rarely flowers and plants. It is all about the symmetry and the vibrant colours.

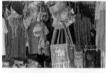

Guilin Embroidery（桂林刺绣）

Guilin embroidery is famous for its **fine stitching** and vibrant colourful renderings of Guilin scenery. More than **130 techniques** are supposedly involved and there are many different stitching styles.

Zhuang Brocade（壮锦）

Zhuang Brocade has its roots in the Han dynasty era of 2000 years ago. The colourful craft pieces incorporate **velvet** and **yarn**, with thick colours, bold lines and a fine weave. Subjects include scenery, people and animals.

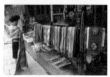

Silk Scarves（丝巾）

Although available all over China, Guilin seems a popular place to buy **silk scarves** of varied patterns and styles, and they make good gifts. Moreover, due to their ubiquity they can be snapped up at very reasonable prices.

Nightlife

In Guilin, the thirsty traveller might try one of the several bars along **Renmin Road** near the **Zhengyang Pedestrian Street**. Meanwhile on **Xixiang**, a small lane near the **Prince's City**, an entrepreneur has opened the **Christmas Bar** next to a church.

Yangshuo's **West Street** and its tributaries, particularly **Xianqian Street** opposite the alley leading to **Monkey Jane's**, are the main party hangouts for most foreign visitors. The scene can be rowdy with live music, free flowing beer and an ever-refreshed crowd of travellers. There are, however, a few options for the more discerning traveller.

Yangshuo Bars

Monkey Jane's

24 Lianfeng Mid-lane, West Street, Yangshuo County 西街南府中卷 24 号（奈也地域村街吧）
Tel:0773-8814086、8820585
Rooftop bar with best views in Yangshuo often hosts games of beer pong choreographed by Monkey Jane herself.

Bad Panda

4F, Lianfeng West Lane, West Street, Yangshuo County 西街主街连华西卷（VB 游吧坐港连卫案一卷）上西糖 1 吸乐 Tel:13814016026
Another West Street rooftop bar with great views but a slightly more mature vibe than Monkey Jane's.

Mojo

The roof of Alishan Hotel, No18 West Street, Yangshuo County 阳朔镇西街 18 号阿里山酒店顶楼 Tel:18778309746
One of the best rooftop bars around West Street.

Rusty Bolt 山色西餐厅

Guihua Bridge, No.102 West Street, Yangshuo County 阳朔县西街 102 号后街桂花街头（阳朔西街原知贵年洁余楼下）
Tel: 18177314499
Popular with the climbing crowd and a good place to pick up tips on local routes and conditions.

Kaya 棵琪酒吧

39 Xianqian Road
Yangshuo's only reggae bar, the hugely popular Kaya now occupies this new location on bar street, upstairs from the Kailai Climbing gear shop.

House Lizard Bar 壁虎酒吧

Near the Ninth warehouse, West Street, Yangshuo County 阳朔招前九号仓库附近 Tel:15078960809
Built to a familiar Bar Street template, this Lizard is a spacious example with live music and dancers.

The Balcony Bar 小马的天

28 Xianqian Rd, Yangshuo County 阳朔镇羊前街 28 号（羊宝街双月部分），Tel:0773-8812331
This back street dive with a tiny terrace facing a small canal has far more atmosphere than most bar street joints, although prices have recently increased.

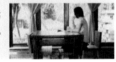

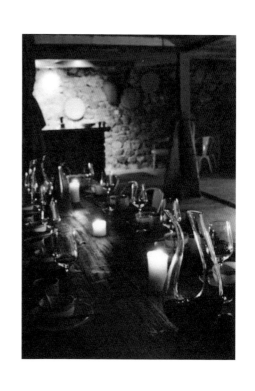

Restaurants and Cafes

The downtown area of Guilin is packed with restaurants where you can try local favourites like Beer Fish, as well as Guilin Rice Noodles, and Li River Crayfish. A good place to sample esoteric local cuisine is the Guilin Snacks Street between Renmin Road and the Zhengyang Pedestrian Street, a covered strip of specialist kiosks and sit down restaurants that serve up appetizing fare.

In Yangshuo, the most vibrant nighttime eating area is around West Street with a few high quality options like **Cloud Nine** as well as a host of lower-priced **Guilin Rice Noodle** places. For a range of international options, including German and Hong Kong style joints, try Yiren Road. There are several attractive options in the countryside around Yangshuo, including courtyard dining at the Giggling Tree in the Yulong river area, and a rustic farmhouse restaurant set above a paddy field in Jiuxian Village.

Typical price for dinner for two
¥ = less than RMB100
¥¥ = RMB100-200
¥¥¥ RMB200+

Guilin

Guilin Rice Noodle Bar
店了粉味

122 Zhengyang Rd, Xiufeng District 桂林市
秀峰区正阳路 122 号；Tel 0773-2807508
This second floor Zhengyang Pedestrian Street
establishment offers not only the area's most
impresive range of Guilin rice noodle dishes
but also home-brewed black beer.

American BBQ and Grill
Renmin Road 桂林秀峰区正阳路

Within staggering distance of the Central
Hostel and Sheraton Hotel, this bar offers the
chance to to kick back with a few beers and
catch up on major league baseball.

Weixiang Restaurant 味香馆

10 Zhengyang Rd,Xiufeng District, 桂林 秀
峰区正阳路 10 号；Tel:18078464219

Venerable establishment on the Zhengyang
Pedestrian Street which is a good place to
sample local snacks such as pumpkin cake
and coconut leaf cakes, while enjoying an Old
Guilin atmosphere.

Bene at 7 贝奈意大利餐厅

7th floor of Sheraton Guilin Hotel
桂林喜来登假日七楼

Tel: 86 773 282 5588

Bene at 7 is located on level 7, riverside by
Lijiang. Well prepared dishes served in this
gorgeous European indoor style will definitely
bring you an unforgettable memories. Open
kitchen allowing you to directly watch the
whole process of making Italian food and
communicate with splendid chef without
limitation. While the unique outdoor terrace
deck which faces the mountain and river is
also a good place to relax and to have some
joyfulness.

Central Kitchen 中央厨房

3 Renmin Rd, Xiufeng District (Near Zhenyang Pedestrian Street, Diagonally opposite of the Sheraton Hotel) 桂林市象山区人民路 3 号; Tel:0773-2819939

The café of the Central Hostel serves up an organic homey vibe, along with its sandwiches, burgers and other western fare. Sundays are 'dumplings' nights, when you may try your hand at making the Chinese festive favourite.

Shanshui Snack Street
山水美食街

Behind Zhenyang Pedestrian Street, Xiufeng District, Guilin
桂林秀峰区正阳步行街内

Running between Renmin Road and the Zhengyang Pedestrian Street, this covered warren of eateries has seating areas and some sit down restaurants. Local delights here include Guihua porridge, tofu rice, ginger duck, sautéed meats, sake-baked crab, and deserts like sweet egg milky flan, date pastries, and tangyuan (sweet dumplings).

Beer Fish Restaurant
漓江啤酒鱼

The beginning of the Zhengyang Pedestrian Street, Xiufeng District, Guilin
桂林秀峰区正阳步行街内；
Tel:15578337165

This unpretentious eatery with outside seating opposite the Central Hostel is not a bad place to sample the famous Beer Fish, on offer for RMB88.

Rosemary Cafe 迷迭香

1-1 Yiren Rd, Xiufeng District, Guilin (inside the Zhenyang Pedestrian Street) 桂林秀峰区依仁路 1-1 号（正阳步行街内）

This comfortable English flavor café on Yiren Road introduces western staples like pizza and steak at reasonable prices, as well as Chinese favourites. Try the chicken and beef burritos.

Paul's Steak House 宝罗牛扒

Xiufeng District, Guilin 桂林秀峰区正阳步行街 77 号 2 楼; Tel:0773-2859987

This steak house with a balcony overlooking Zhengyang Pedestrian Street impresses with its 18 choices of meat cuts.

Elephant Cafe 象·咖啡

Next to the Gate 1 of Elephant Park, Xiufeng District, Guilin 桂林秀峰区象山公园一号口旁票厅旁; Tel:0773-3899686

Sausages are the specialty of this riverside cafe sat at the start of the ascent to the Elephant Hill with the wide choice including Swiss cervelet, roasted nueremberger, and frankfurters.

Kali Mirch (black pepper) Indian Cuisine 黑胡椒印度餐厅

15 Binjiang Street, (Shanshui Street behind the Sheraton) Xiufeng District, Guilin
桂林秀峰区滨江路 15 号;
Tel: 13737396451.

Email: kali_mirch@yahoo.cn

Promising to "Spice up your travel experience" Kali Mirch is a colourful eatery specialising in homemade paneer (cottage cheese) and yogurt. The all-Indian kitchen staff use traditional charcoal fires to ensure the authentic taste of India is delivered in style to South China.

Nengren Zhaiguan 能仁斋馆

6 Lijun Rd, Xiufeng District, Guilin
桂林市秀峰区丽君路 6 号

The Nengren Temple on Lijun Road is one of the city's few Buddhist enclaves. It's a pretty place, home to 14 monks. Once you've paid your respects in the Grand Buddha Hall and the Goddess of Mercy Temple, check out the affiliated Nengren Vegetarian Restaurant, the first pure veggie eatery in Guilin. RMB26 will gain unlimited access to a buffet dinner, including salad bar, faux meat, meat-free dumplings, tea, juice and other vegan delights.

Yangshuo

Le Votre 乐得法式餐厅

79 West street, Yangshuo County. 阳 朔 镇 西街 79 号 ; Tel:0773-8828040
Prestigious French run hotel and restaurant in central West Street, offering French classics such as Escargots a la Francaise (RMB50), while other specialties include stewed chicken (RMB45). The restaurant also hits the spot with its bacon and eggs breakfast.

Cloud 9 望福楼

1 Chengzhong Rd, West Street, Yangshuo County.
阳朔镇西街城中路 1 号 ; Tel:0773-8813686
Classy Sichuanese joint which serves up a good spread from all over China. The Li River Poached Fish is fresh, and the Taro and Pork Stew also comes recommended. More exotic menu options for the adventurous include Dog Hotpot and Bamboo Rat.

Snow Lion

1 Mushan Village, Yangshuo County(Near to Impress Liusanjie) 阳朔县木山村 1 号 (此 谷临 象刘 三姐 剧场); Tel:13507838851
Snow Lion wows with a wide range of western foods, and local specialties like Beer Fish and River Snail Wine (田 螺 酿). The restaurant also has a pool that customers may use.

Xie San Jie 谢二姐啤酒鱼

Inside Sunshine100, Diecui Rd, Yangshuo County(near to Furong crossing).
阳朔县叠翠路阳光 100 内 (近芙蓉路口), Tel:0773-8820577
A dependable Chinese restaurant with local favourites like Beer Fish (RMB88/1/2kg), Li River Shrimp (RMB80/ 1/2kg), and Farm Crispy Chicken.

Rosewood Cafe 玫瑰木餐厅

83 West Street, Yangshuo County
阳 朔 西街 83 号 (近 鹏 海 鹏 餐 贸 城),

Tel:0773-8827953
The restaurant inside the Rosewood Hotel serves solid food in a table-clothed environment. The breakfast buffet for 48RMB is a popular choice for those in search of a western breakfast.

Giggling Tree 格格树饭店

Aishanmen Village, Yangshuo County
阳朔镇地门门口; Tel:13661266754
Guests and visitors may both enjoy al-fresco dining in the courtyard of this hotel near the Yulong River. The western and Chinese menu ranges from specials like snake, snail or rabbit, to the humble toasted cheese sandwich.

Lao Hu Jia 老胡家二洛鱼

71 Guihua Rd, Yangshuo County(Near to Xie San Jie Beer Fish) 阳朔桂花路 71 号 (靠茶婆与桂花路交界处, 距漓江路 150 米)(近谢三姐啤酒鱼店对足 100 步远), Tel: 0773-8824099
Two branches of the popular Lao Hu Jia restaurant sit opposite each other on Guihua Road. One specializes in dumplings and Guilin Rice Noodles, the other entices with dishes like baked sword fish (88/jin) and Lijiang Ginger duck .

German Oak Restaurant & Bar 德国餐厅

83 West Street, Yangshuo County
阳朔西街 83 号 (光荣购物街商城);
Tel:0773-8827953
If you crave German food, this restaurant in the centre of things puts everything in order with its chicken schnitzel burgers (RMB68), German made sausages (RMB78) and wide range of Teutonic beers (RMB45 up.)

Lung Kee Beer Fish

Guihua Road.
The Lung Kee Beer Fish Restaurant (since 1991)

147

is a refreshingly humble café for this stretch of Guihua Road, and has other options like Hong Kong milk tea, stewed carp and Bamboo Fish.

Primitive House
原始人

34 West Street, Yangshuo County
阳朔西街 34 号 Tel:0773-8827744
Highly popular with westerners craving home comforts who visit Primitive House for its roast chicken, ribs, apple crumble and superior cheesecake.

'First Under Heaven' Guilin Rice Noodle 老詹天下第一桂林米粉

Sunshine 100 on Furong Rd, Yangshuo County 阳朔县芙蓉路阳光 100 后街楼（起 香芙路）: Tel:18777338022.
The self-annointed 'First Under Heaven' of Guilin Rice Noodles, this admittedly bustling joint also serves up other popular local snacks like fried dough sticks, taro cakes, and sticky rice dumplings.

Furong Rice Noodle 芙蓉米粉店

7 Furong Rd, Yangshuo County 阳朔芙蓉路 7 号（近车站前）: Tel 13977331645
Another Guilin Rice Noodle specialist which occupies a shady spot near the county government on Furong Road.

Shouzi Guilin Noodles
瘦子桂林米粉（城中路）

Chengzhong Rd, Yangshuo County
阳朔县城中路（近膏菜路、宝光塔口）:
Tel:13978397389
This unpretentious Yangshuo institution is a favourite with locals as well as visitors for its slender Guilin noodles. Customers sit on wooden benches and the noodles are served up in enamel bowls.

UBC Coffee
上岛咖啡

2nd F, 117 West Street, Yangshuo County

阳朔西街 117 号 2 楼；Tel:0773-8828897
The West Street branch of the popular Chinese coffee chain ticks most boxes with its combo of a large Chinese style menu, and reliable wifi.

Pizzeria Corner 披萨小街

3 Guihua Road, Yangshuo County.
阳朔桂花路 3 号；Tel: 0773 8821065
This street corner eatery has an open kitchen, affordable wood baked pizza (RMB35-45) and outdoor seating.

Echo Cafe

Next to the county government, 2 Fuqian Lane, Yangshuo County 阳朔府前巷 2 号（县政府旁）: Tel: 14795933633
Away from the hustle and bustle of West Street, this cosy German-run café offers imported beer and home cooked food. Echo also hosts occasional film nights and music.

Ganga Impression
恒河印象印度餐厅

110B, Block D, Yangguang 100, Yangshuo County 阳光阳光 100D 座 100B 号;
Tel: 0773-8811456.
Email: gangaimpression@qq.com
Well-located Indian restaurant, with friendly and professional management and a comprehensive menu of high-quality South Asian cuisine.

The Old Street Cafe
兴坪七号小店

7 Old Street, Xingping Town, Yangshuo County 阳朔兴平镇 兴坪 老 街 7 号;
Tel:15977009927.
Operated by a kindly pair of English-speaking sisters from nearby Fuli, this backpacker-friendly eatery in the heart of old Xingping offers a broad choice of Western and Chinese food (including seriously good homemade chili sauce). The photos on the walls are those of Gregory Michiels, a Xingping based photographer and guide.

148

Master Café 吴坪当戏台咖啡厅

Near to Warm Cafe, Xingping,Yangshuo County 即桂兴坪老街（温馨餐吧附近）

This café on Xingping Old Street serves blue mountain coffee and snacks like squid and American hot dog, but the main attraction is an old building tastefully restored with period features like ceiling beams and latticed windows.

Hostelling International Restaurant

Near the Old Street arch entrance from the river.

This establishment near the river-side entrance to Xingping Old Street occupies a beautiful old slanted-roof courtyard style town house and serves up a range of western and Chinese dishes, including Beer Dragon Fish for RMB88.

Warm Cafe 温馨餐吧

53 Old Street, Xingping,Yangshuo County 即桂兴坪老街 53 号；Tel:13457362870

This cosy little cafe charms travellers from afar with English menus featuring inexpensive Chinese staples like Spicy Tofu, soups, and western faves like pizza and smoothies.

Little Hours Cafe 旧时旧刻咖啡

86 Jiuxian Village,Baisha Town ,Yangshuo County 即阳朔白沙镇旧县 86 号；Tel:13878376678

A small café which conveniently marks the turn-off to Jiuxian Village, Little Hours offers reasonably priced coffees, teas, and freshly-squeezed mango and passion fruit juices.

Lao Gen Far Restaurant
老根农家饭店

Jiuxian Village,Yangshuo County 即阳朔县 旧村内；Tel:0773-8772715

Raised on stilts above a paddy field close to the village entrance, this rustic restaurant specializes in organic chicken dishes – you probably saw your dinner running around on the street earlier -prepared in the farmhouse opposite. Fresh vegetable dishes also use local produce.

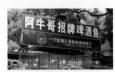

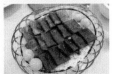

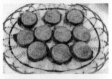

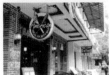

Shops

Guilin is a city where most conveniences of modern life can be easily procured. The tourist hub around **Zhengyang Pedestrian Street** boasts a cluster of convenience stores, banks and clothes stores. You will find banks with ATMs, including a convenient outlet of the **China Construction Bank**. On the nearby city artery of Jiefang Road are department stores like the **Wancheng Department Store** and travel agencies that sell tickets and tours. Opposite the Rosemary Café on Libin Road is a pharmacy.

Yangshuo's West Street has a large number of tourism related outlets selling osmanthus cakes and other local products. A major mall is noisily under construction at the north end of the street. However, there are several small supermarkets in the surrounding streets. You may also find cause to visit specialist shops selling useful gear like **Bike Asia** at 8 Guihua Road and the climbing gear outlet which shares premises with **Kailas bar** at 39 Xianqian Street.

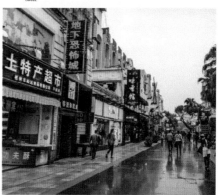

Useful Numbers

Police	110
Guilin Police	0773-2823334
Guilin Travel Gov	0773-2825890
Guilin Tourist Information Centre	0773-2800318
Guilin International Tourism Management Office	0773-2827643
Directory Enquiries	114
Ambulance	120
Fire Service	119
Weather Forecast	12121
Air Ticketing	2581
Railway Information	2585
China International Travel Service	86-10-65222991

Useful Websites

CNVOL.com (China train schedules in English) http://www.cnvol.com/
Ctrip.com International (Largest website for China hotels and flights) http://english.ctrip.com/
China Tourist Maps http://www.chinatouristmaps.com/
Travel China Guide(Train and flight schedules.).) http://www.travelchinaguide.com
China International Travel Service http://www.cits.net/

Useful Phrases

Hello	nihao (nee how)
Goodbye	zaijian (dzayjenn)
Please	qing (cheeng)
Do you speak English?	ni hui yingwen ma? (nee whey Eeng-win ma?)
I'm sorry	duibuqi (dway-boo-chee)
Yes	shi (shir)
No	bu (boo)
Excuse me	qing wen (cheeng wen)
How much is that?	duoshaoqian? (daw-show-chyen?)
How do I get to…?	dao…zenmezou? (dow…dzummadzow?)

INDEX

153

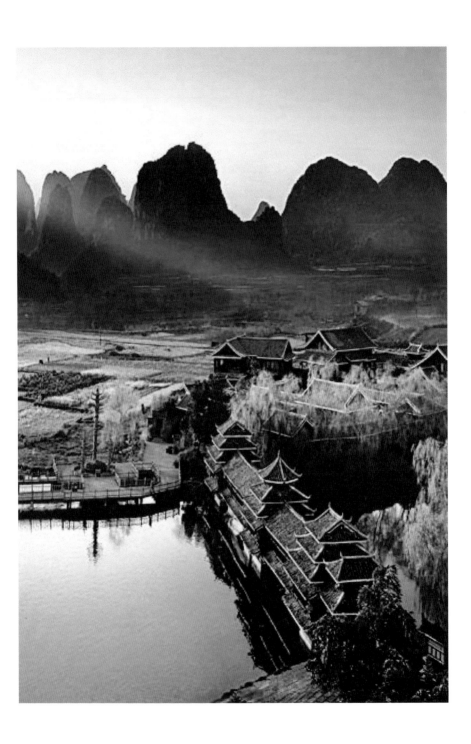

12144777R00095

Printed in Germany
by Amazon Distribution
GmbH, Leipzig